# WHAT SORT OF NHS
# DO WE WANT?

By David Taylor-Gooby

ISBN: 978-1-907720-60-4

Typeset and designed by Deirdré Gyenes

# WHAT SORT OF NHS DO WE WANT?

By David Taylor-Gooby

## About the author

DAVID TAYLOR-GOOBY lives in Peterlee County Durham with his wife Maureen. He is a life-long member of the Labour Party and has been involved with it in various ways, and has served on the National Policy Forum and the Regional Board.

David was a district councillor in Easington for twenty years, and previously served as a parish councillor in a County Durham village. He was a member of the Board of East Durham Homes for eight years, serving for a period as chair. He is also Chair of the Apollo Pavilion Community Association.

He was a senior lecturer at East Durham College, and ran the Health Studies Degree course in conjunction with the University of Sunderland. He later worked for the Commission for Public and Patient Involvement in Health, and completed a research project on public involvement at the university with Dr Stephen MacDonald. He also served on Durham County Council's Health Overview and Scrutiny Committee. He is currently a Lay Member of the Durham Dales, Easington and Sedgefield Commissioning Group.

David has thought a great deal about how both local government and the NHS can more effectively involve the public. This book is the result of his ideas, and the views expressed are entirely his own, and not those of any of the organisations with which he is associated.

## About Searching Finance

Searching Finance publishes and curates economics, finance and politics.
Follow us on Facebook at www.facebook.com/searchingfinance
Our website is: www.searchingfinance.com

# CONTENTS

# PREFACE

I HAVE been involved with both local government and the NHS for a long time. I am a firm believer that both are an integral part of the society we live in, and Britain would not be a good society if either were allowed to decline or even disappear.

We live in a society where commercial and market values have been allowed to dominate for some time, and the public appear to be sickening of them and realising their limitations. Both local government and the NHS express values of community and solidarity, of us all having mutual obligations which challenge an individualistic market-dominated view of the world.That is why I have spent much of my life working with both.

It is not enough, however, simply to say how wonderful these institutions are, and leave it at that. Nor should we immediately oppose any attempt to modernise them or make them fit for purpose. What we must do, however, is have clear ideas of how the NHS can continue to survive with the increasing demands being made on it, and also how local government can be involved with it and engage with the public more that it does now. I have set out a few idea sin this book which I hope others will develop and debate.

This is not meant to be a partisan document, although I have made my own views, as a Christian Socialist, clear throughout. I want all those who believe in both the NHS and local government to debate the ideas put forward here, and develop a vision of how we should go forward. Much political debate is necessarily short-term. What I want to develop here is a longer term vision.

I must conclude with thanking Maureen, without whose support, encouragement and constructive criticism this book would never have happened. I owe a debt of gratitude too to the collected philosophers and comedians of Peterlee Swimming baths who keep me going and in touch with reality.

# CHAPTER 1

# INTRODUCTION

THERE IS A VILLAGE near where I live with a population of just over 5,000. It was established as a colliery, but the pit closed in 1981. The signs of economic decline are rather obvious, but what strikes you most when you walk down the Front Street is the number of fast food outlets – six at the last count, with two shops which concentrate on cheap alcohol. There are also two large care homes.

Here in microcosm are the problems facing our health service. Economic decline has brought bad health and the resulting bad habits. There is also a large, and growing, population of the elderly for whom care has to be provided. It seems to present an enormous challenge.

But things are not as bad as they appear at first. There are many good people in the village who are trying to do something about the situation. There is a lively health centre, with innovative and dedicated GPs and a go-ahead manager. There is a thriving garden association which has 250 gardens and a waiting list. It provides fresh vegetables which are sold at the community centre.

The community centre itself has been proactive in attracting funding, and now runs a range of activities. Currently, over 350 people of all ages use a wide variety of services at the centre including healthy living activities such as skipping, indoor bowls, tea dances and line dancing, keyboard classes, IT classes, drama workshops, cake decorating and art classes, plus a fitness suite and a community café. The latest addition is Pilates. They also have a lively WI. The reason I know so much about the place is that they invited me down to speak. Hope they got over it.

What impressed me most about the community, however, is the Health Forum. This was originally set up by the Primary Care Trust, but funding has now been cut. They originally had professional help, but they now run it themselves and have managed to secure funding from various sources. It received a small grant which it used as leverage to attract additional funding, and then distributed it to projects which promoted good health. In the past, it has supported various schemes, including a project to install low-level lighting in senior citizens' homes to minimise the risk of falls, outdoor ventures for the cadets and other youth groups, and an allotment. The actual spending of the money was properly monitored. All this was done by volunteers who cared about their community and its health.

So there is hope. A community which has been on the sharp end of recession and economic decline, and has experienced their effects at first hand, is doing something about it.

It made me think. What sort of role do we see for the NHS in the future? We frequently hear about the health risks of bad lifestyles, and how conditions such as obesity are likely to increase. We have managed to tame smoking, but alcohol abuse shows no sign of abating. The NHS will be financially constrained whichever government is in power, and we cannot expect it to solve all our problems alone. Communities must do something to help.

In this book I attempt to set out my ideas about how a community-based, democratically run health service will function in the future. If we are to deal with bad health, it is a job for all of us. Despite our problems, we have some examples of very good practice here in the North East where I live, and I want to draw on these to define my vision.

Nigel Lawson once said that the NHS was the nearest thing we had to a national religion.[1] In many ways it is similar to our other supposed national religion, the Anglican Church, which people want to be there if they need it. It is true that people in this country remain very attached to the NHS, but we have to think hard about how it is going to cope fairly and effectively in the years ahead when resources will be constrained. That is a challenge for all of us.

The controversial Health and Social Care Act[2] is now law. There has been tremendous opposition to it, mainly due to the perceived threat of large-scale privatisation, and the breaking up of what is regarded as a national treasure. At the next election, a future government will be faced with the situation of having to work with the consequences of the new Act. Simply repealing it will not solve the problems faced by the NHS. Peter Watt, former general secretary of the Labour Party, commented: "Back to the future is hardly an inspirational rallying cry for Labour. Instead it needs to begin to set out what its vision for the NHS is." (*The Guardian*, March 21st 2012)

This book is a contribution to that debate from one who passionately loves the NHS, but feels it must evolve and become more community-based. I hope you find it interesting, and it gives you an idea of what sort of health service we could have in this country in the future.

# CHAPTER 2
# THE PRINCIPLES UNDERLYING
# THE NHS

*The NHS is important and we want it to succeed. This chapter recognises that before we can define policies for the future of the NHS, we must have some idea, some vision, of what a "good" NHS would look like. To this end we seek to identify values which underpin it, and objectives which it should have.*

I FIRST CONSULTED the 2012 edition of the NHS Constitution.[3] Its opening statement is as follows:

> "The NHS belongs to the people. It is there to improve our health and well-being, supporting us to keep mentally and physically well, to get better when we are ill and, when we cannot fully recover, to stay as well as we can to the end of our lives. It works at the limits of science – bringing the highest levels of human knowledge and skill to save lives and improve health. It touches our lives at times of basic human need, when care and compassion are what matter most. The NHS is founded on a common set of principles and values which bind together the communities and people it serves – patients and public – and the staff who work for it."

It then sets out the principles which guide the NHS. I have just written down the headings here – they are followed by explanations.

# Principles that guide the NHS

1. The NHS provides a comprehensive service, available to all.

2. Access to NHS services is based on clinical need, not an individual's ability to pay.

3. The NHS aspires to the highest standards of excellence and professionalism.

4. NHS services must reflect the needs and preferences of patients, their families and their carers.

5. The NHS works across organisational boundaries and in partnership with other organisations in the interest of patients, local communities and the wider population.

6. The NHS is committed to providing best value for taxpayers' money and the most effective, fair and sustainable use of finite resources.

7. The NHS is accountable to the public, communities and patients that it serves.

At the end of the document is a set of values which underpin these principles.

## Values

*Respect and dignity.* We value each person as an individual, respect their aspirations and commitments in life, and seek to understand their priorities, needs, abilities and limits. We take what others have to say seriously. We are honest about our point of view and what we can and cannot do.

*Commitment to quality of care.* We earn the trust placed in us by insisting on quality and striving to get the basics right every time: safety, confidentiality, professional and managerial integrity, accountability, dependable service and good communication. We welcome feedback, learn from our mistakes and build on our successes.

*Compassion.* We respond with humanity and kindness to each person's pain, distress, anxiety or need. We search for the things we can do, however small, to give comfort and relieve suffering. We find time for those we serve and work alongside. We do not wait to be asked, because we care.

*Improving lives.* We strive to improve health and well-being and people's experiences of the NHS. We value excellence and professionalism wherever we find it – in the everyday things that make people's lives better as much as in clinical practice, service improvements and innovation.

*Working together for patients.* We put patients first in everything we do, by reaching out to staff, patients, carers, families, communities, and professionals outside the NHS. We put the needs of patients and communities before organisational boundaries.

*Everyone counts.* We use our resources for the benefit of the whole community, and make sure nobody is excluded or left behind. We accept that some people need more help, that difficult decisions have to be taken – and that when we waste resources we waste others' opportunities. We recognise that we all have a part to play in making ourselves and our communities healthier.

*(NHS Constitution, Department of Health, 2012)*

## Responsibility and accountability

Many of these are principles and values which no civilised person could disagree with, but what strikes me are two things: first, that it involves everyone – it is accountable to "the community" (principle 7); and second, that it can only succeed if it works in a cooperative and collective way – that it works across organisational boundaries and in partnership with other organisations (principle 5).

The quasi-Troskyist introduction actually states that "The NHS belongs to the people".

The first principle of the Constitution of the World Health Organisation [4] states: "Health is a state of complete physical, mental and social well-being and not merely the absence of disease or infirmity."

From this it would appear that good health is not just the responsibility of a health service, but other agencies as well. Thus, to revisit the opening paragraph of the NHS Constitution, which states: "It is there to improve our health and well-being, supporting us to keep mentally and physically well, to get better when we are ill and, when we cannot fully recover, to stay as well as we can to the end of our lives." From this it is difficult for the NHS to see itself as simply an organisation on its own, but rather as part of a wider collective which must work with other agencies in society if it is to succeed.

## Health inequalities

No more is this obvious as in the case of health inequalities. These were brought to the fore in 1979 with the publication of the Black Report. This stated baldly that, despite rising standards of health overall after 30 years of the NHS, inequalities in health persisted. There has been a succession of reports since, culminating in the Marmot Report of 2010 'Fair Society, Healthy Lives'.[5] Despite some individual success stories, such as reducing inequalities in child health, the inequalities have persisted and even grown in some cases.

The findings of the Marmot Report can be summarised as follows:

- People living in the poorest neighbourhoods in England will on average die seven years earlier than people living in the richest neighbourhoods.

- People living in poorer areas not only die sooner, but spend more of their lives with disability – an average total difference of 17 years.

- The Review highlights the social gradient of health inequalities – put simply, the lower one's social and economic status, the poorer one's health is likely to be.

- Health inequalities arise from a complex interaction of many factors – housing, income, education, social isolation, disability – all of which are strongly affected by one's economic and social status.

- Health inequalities are largely preventable. Not only is there a strong social justice case for addressing health inequalities, there is also a pressing economic case. It is estimated that the annual cost of health inequalities is between £36 billion and £40 billion through lost taxes, welfare payments and costs to the NHS.

- Action on health inequalities requires action across all the social determinants of health, including education, occupation, income, home and community.

It is clear that health inequalities are the result of a complex mixture of social, economic and genetic and personal factors. These inequalities are not mentioned in the NHS Constitution. Reference to them only appeared in the Health and Social Care Bill after amendment in the House of Lords.[6]

## The changing role of public health

Health inequalities are now seen as the responsibility of public health, which is to be transferred to local government (under the present proposals) so they need not be addressed in a document about the principles of the NHS. There are good reasons why public health should become part of local government. It is beneficial that public health agencies work with other local government departments. But is essentially still part of the overall health service, and should not be seen as something distinct from the NHS. Concern for health inequalities should be throughout the NHS.

The role of public health has changed. The original pioneers in the 19th century were concerned with clean water and healthy sanitation so as to prevent disease. John Snow, who started work as a doctor in County Durham, became famous for removing the handle from an infected water pump in Broad Street, London in 1854, and Edwin Chadwick was the first director of the Board of

Public Health in 1848 which worked to improve sanitation, and therefore stopping the source of a cholera outbreak. The London County Council had its origins in a body to provide clean water and lay proper sewers. There is a very good description of these early pioneers in the book 'The New Public Health'. [7] As Professor Ashton points out in the book, these things are still important, but taken for granted. The emphasis now is more towards encouraging healthy lifestyles. It is therefore essential that public health be integrated with other aspects of the NHS.

The current literature about the new structures is remarkably coy about health inequalities. Nowhere is there a specific statement that health inequalities are undesirable and should be reduced as far as is possible. The recent White Paper "Healthy Lives, Healthy People" [8] deals with the problem in a rather evasive way. In the introduction it states:

> "Health inequalities in life expectancy and disability-free life expectancy are large. We know that a wide range of factors affect people's health throughout their life and drive inequalities such as early years care, housing and social isolation. Despite this, our health efforts focus much more on treatment than on the causes of poor health. The NHS spends over £2.7 billion a year on treating smoking related illness, but less than £150 million on smoking cessation."

And later:

> "Healthy Lives, Healthy People: Our strategy for public health in England will work to re-balance the focus on the causes of ill health and ensure that public health funding is prioritised and not squeezed by other pressures ... This is potentially one of the great challenges of our generation – how we can create a public health service, not just a national sickness service."

Although a "wide range of factors" is acknowledged to cause these health inequalities, the emphasis is very much on people and communities making healthier choices – an individualistic emphasis. There is not the stress on working together that there is in the NHS Constitution, or in the Marmot Report.

It is not the case that health inequalities are not mentioned at all in the literature about the new NHS arrangements, just that they do not have the same emphasis and prominence as they did before. For example, Race for Health, the NHS-based programme that works to drive forward improvements in health for people from black, and minority ethnic backgrounds, puts the emphasis on race and ethnic inequalities in its 2011 publication 'Tackling Health Inequalities in the New NHS'.

Compare, however, the rather evasive language of 'Healthy Lives, Healthy People' with the introduction to 'Tackling Health Inequalities: A Programme for Action' (Department of Health, 2003):[9]

> "But it's not all a story of unrelenting and welcome advances. Our society remains scarred by inequalities. Whole communities remain cut off from the greater wealth and opportunities that others take for granted. This, in turn, fuels avoidable health inequalities.
>
> The statistics are shocking enough ... Social justice demands action.
>
> Tackling such entrenched and enduring health inequalities is, of course, a daunting challenge ...
>
> We have started to tackle this health gap, not least by the sustained and record investment in the NHS and our other vital public services. More fundamentally, a whole series of cross-departmental action will address the root causes of poor health and health inequalities. This Programme for Action builds on successes like Sure Start, our smoking cessation services and the teenage pregnancy strategy.
>
> We also need to recognise that continued success in tackling health inequalities requires the courage to work in new ways. It means setting national standards for services but giving those responsible for delivering on the ground the freedom locally to meet these standards ...

We need diverse, rather than identical, solutions which can only come from giving communities and front-line staff the power to redesign, refocus and reprioritise programmes to tackle local need."

This was signed off by Tony Blair.

It would be foolhardy to suggest that health inequalities can be totally eliminated. They are caused by a mixture of social conditions, lifestyle, generic inheritance, and economic pressures. (Healthy people are more likely to leave a poor area more readily than less healthy ones, for example, thus skewing the statistics.) Nevertheless as Wilkinson and Pickett point out in 'The Spirit Level' [10] they are much greater in some societies than others, and those where they are least tend to be better societies in other ways. The other point is that, to a large extent, they are avoidable. Should a commitment to trying to reduce health inequalities be a core principle of the NHS? It seems to me that, for a Labour government at least, the result is an overwhelming "yes."

## Defining NHS core values

It is now time to try and define what our core values for the NHS should be. Perhaps it would help the debate to construct a continuum with an individualistic approach at one end, and a collective one at the other.

Individualistic                                    Collective

|_____|

Thus a system where individuals were entirely responsible for their own healthcare, purchasing it when and where required, would be a purely individualistic system. Government would play little or no part in promoting public health. Aspects of such an approach exist in parts of the United States, although I should stress it is different in different states. Smoking bans in California are tougher than here.

Alternatively a situation where the state controlled all healthcare and determined what sort of care an individual could have would be entirely collectivist. An example could be Romania under Ceaucescu when abortions were denied. In actual practice we are not looking for pure examples of either. The continuum is simply a measure where we can place different systems which exist in the real world.

Consider the present state of the current English system. At the time of writing, the reforms instigated by the coalition government have not taken effect. Thus there are currently individualist elements. "Patient Choice" is individualistic, and allows individuals to choose the hospitals and treatment they want. If there is more private provision, as is proposed, then this aspect of our system will grow. It is important to note, however, that in a medical context choice has to be properly informed.

On the other hand, the funding of the system is collective, not individualistic. Private health insurance only plays a minor role. All pay in, and all use the service. There is no system of refund if you do not use it, and most do. Similarly, aspects of public health are collective, most notably the smoking ban in public places. This is a measure which restricts individual liberty for the sake of the common good.

The whole concept of "everyone counts", which is referred to in the NHS Constitution, Value 6, does seem to be collective: "We use our resources for the benefit of the whole community, and make sure nobody is excluded or left behind", and "We recognise that we all have a part to play in making ourselves and our communities healthier".

Policies to tackle health inequalities are necessarily also a collectivist approach. The whole community acts to remedy what are essentially the problems of individuals. The whole concept of inequalities recognises a wider society within which these inequalities exist. A totally individualistic perspective would not think inequalities to be important.

Principle 5 in the Constitution also has a collectivist approach: "The NHS works across organisational boundaries and in partnership with other organisations in the interest of patients, local communities and the wider population."

Thus, on balance, the NHS has more collectivist than individualist aspects. The social policy writer Norman Ginsberg once described England as a "liberal collectivist" society[11] – we value our freedoms, but still do things together. Perhaps the NHS reflects this apparent contradiction.

The NHS constitution also stresses accountability. Principle 7 states: "The NHS is accountable to the public, communities and patients that it serves."

This assumes a collective approach – that the NHS is accountable to communities. It is not a series of individual transactions. The mechanisms for accountability are complex. Overall the NHS is accountable to parliament. Individual trusts have systems of governance which involve the wider public to a greater or a lesser degree. Local authorities have democratically elected members. 'Third sector' organisations have various systems. There are also organisations which promote patient and public involvement.

Current concerns about accountability often concentrate on financial and managerial systems. Thus Monitor, the regulator of Foundation Trusts, was able to give Mid Staffordshire NHS Trust a clean bill of health when patients were dying.[12] Proper accountability must also involve the users of the service. This episode highlights the conflict between professional and market values, when value for money is emphasised at the expense of other concerns.

We shall return to this complex jungle later.

To conclude therefore, we shall identify some basic principles for the NHS which will guide us in describing what it should look like. These are:

- As far as possible patients should have choice, but choice has to be properly informed.

- Health is a collective responsibility for the whole of society.

- Health is a state of wellbeing, not simply the absence of illness.

- Good health is the result of a complex range of factors, not all medical.

- All organisations responsible for ensuring good health should cooperate as far as possible.

- Services ensuring good health should provide the best value for money (this should apply to any public service).

- The incidence of health inequalities should be reduced as far as is practical.

- Services promoting good health should be accountable to patients, the public and the wider community.

- Finally we have to remember the mantra with which the constitution begins: "The NHS belongs to the people". We want an NHS which we all feel part of, which is both democratically run, but involves volunteers effectively and takes them seriously. In the future, people will work with professionals, not simply be told what to do.

The emphasis of these principles is collective, although it contains aspects of individualism, which is a tension running through much of this country's life. People nowadays have more freedom of choice and are not required to conform in the way they once were. Nevertheless people value a sense of collective identity, of togetherness. The NHS is one of the few institutions where we now express these values.

In the reminder of this book I intend to construct a vision of what an NHS based on these values might look like. However, ideas have little value if they are impractical, so I shall draw on aspects of good practice in the North East of England, before attempting to set out a blueprint of what the NHS should ideally look like in the future.

*This chapter finds that there is a strong collective sense in the ideas and principles of the NHS. Health is the responsibility of all of us. The same feeling was expressed by the last government regarding health inequalities, with a strong emphasis on the responsibility of society to deal with them. There is less emphasis on a collective responsibility for tackling these inequalities in the proposals of the present government, which seems to favour a more individualistic approach.*

*It is accepted that there should be patient choice, partly as a way of ensuring good treatment, although choice in health has to be informed. This along with the strong belief in a collective approach emphasises the English commitment to "liberal collectivism", which believes in both individual freedom and collective values.*

*Public support and affection for the NHS is precisely because it does express fundamentally national concerns.*

# CHAPTER 3

# WHAT THE NHS IS LIKE NOW

*This chapter looks at how the NHS has developed since in started in 1948, and considers some of the sociological and managerial literature which analyses these developments. The challenges facing the NHS now are very different from when it was first established, and how the NHS is organised has changed, partly influenced by the changes in other large-scale organisations. There is now a more commercial approach than hitherto, and more delegation to individual units.*

*The current debate about privatisation and the future of the NHS sometimes appears to assume the NHS is still organised the way it was in Aneurin Bevan's time. This is not the case. It has developed from an organisation with the specific role of treating illness into the contemporary concept of something which ensures we are healthy, or 'health management'. The contemporary NHS has evolved into a commissioning service with multi-agency working, with third sector involvement now commonplace.*

*The focus on best value from services has transformed patients to customers and has led to an increase in target-led services. As will be shown in this chapter, the development of a market-based NHS has put much more emphasis on feedback and assessment of the quality of the service. This could be seen as more involvement of the public and patients as consumers, but it is not the same as them influencing how it works.*

# The development of the modern NHS

When the NHS was established in 1948 it incorporated a variety of institutions, all with their own forms of governance and connections with the public. Some hospitals were run by local authorities, others by charities and bodies such as trades unions. There were also the remnants of the Poor Law which persisted up until 1948 (Timmins, 1995;[13] Webster, 2002[14]). What we now understand as the primary care aspects of the NHS, i.e. maternity and child welfare, district nursing, health centres and community health, continued to be organised by local authorities until the reforms of 1974. Thus a whole range of connections with the public, either through local boards, elected councils or even voluntary groups involved in fundraising, was eliminated when the centrally controlled NHS was established. Aneurin Bevan even boasted that "the sound of a dropped bedpan in Tredegar would reverberate around the Palace of Westminster" (Glasby et al, 2007[15]).

The prevailing philosophy at the time was that a strong central approach was the way to get things done. This had been the approach in the war, and continued after it. The National Coal Board, the National Grid, and even the 'new towns' such as Peterlee are good examples.

The priority at the time was dealing with epidemics and putting right the ravages of the war.

Thus the NHS concentrated on hospitals and set up a system whereby they were run by regional boards and management committees with some local government involvement. Although local authorities complained about their loss of influence, much medical opinion thought leaving them with primary care and community services and not transferring these services to the NHS was a retrograde step (Timmins, 1995; Webster, 2002). Sir George Godber, future Chief Medical Officer of Health, commented that these services would lose out. There was not much enthusiasm at the time for public involvement (Timmins, 1995; Webster, 2002).

The main focus of attention was hospitals rather than health in the wider sense (Hunter et al, 2010[16]). Many argue this is still the case today.

The next significant reforms, those of the Conservative Government in 1974, placed all health services under the control of Health Authorities, although welfare and social services remained with local authorities (Timmins, 1995). A third of these new authorities consisted of councillors, so as to maintain the link with local government. At the same time local government itself was being reorganised following the recommendations of the Redcliffe Maud Commission (Elcock, 1994[17]). A major change in 1974 was the establishment of Community Health Councils (CHCs). These were intended to represent the public interest and included councillors (Timmins. 1995).

The performance of the CHCs varied, but they continued until the 2001 Health and Social Care Act and the establishment of the Commission for Patient and Public Involvement in Health (CPPIH) in January 2003. The 2001 changes were made against the background of major changes in the NHS. The idea of an internal market had been introduced into the NHS (Henderson, 2001[19]; Martin *et al,* 2010[20]). Healthcare was now commissioned by Primary Care Trusts from the independently-run hospitals, which eventually became Foundation Trusts. The involvement organisations shadowed these distinct trusts, rather than covering geographical areas. Who was responsible for what became less clear to the public.

The way the NHS has been managed has also changed. The old idea as enunciated by Aneurin Bevan in 1948 was very much a centrally controlled organisation, as were other newly nationalised organisations at the time. There was immediately a tension with demands for local involvement by local authorities and the public and patients, as alluded to above. These tensions will be explored further in the next chapter. I shall now look briefly at what sociological theory can tell us about how the NHS is run.

# Management theory and public sector organisations

Sociological management theory was originally defined within the work of Max Weber. Weber defined organisation structure where there was a hierarchy, where promotion was on merit, and each position had clearly defined duties as a 'bureaucracy' (Weber, 1947[21]; Du Gay, 2000[22]; Miner, 2007[23]). Although the word 'bureaucratic' now has bad overtones, particularly when used by Conservative MPs, the development of efficient bureaucracies led to considerable advances in human welfare and happiness. Writing in early 20th century Germany, Weber based his ideas on the efficient organisations which followed military lines created by Bismarck. Such a system could produce a large number of products efficiently – an example being the US and UK car industries, where the philosophy became known as 'Fordism'. This model of management underpinned the concept of early 20th century capitalism (Handy, 1999[24]; Wood and Wood, 2002[25]), and was also adopted by communist and fascist countries.

Yet, as Hoggett [26] suggests, contemporary organisations have evolved into far more complex structures due to globalisation and should be conceptualised through the notion of 'post-Fordism'. This is due to their complex nature, where rigid bureaucracy along Weberian lines is no longer viable, and has to be replaced with a decentralised system with an emphasis on outcomes rather than rules.

Ahough the old Weberian hierarchy may be less evident, post-Fordist power relationships still remain as a mechanism of keeping costs under control (Bolton, 2004[27]). Peter Drucker, the 20th century management theorist, developed ideas about the public sector during his life. One of his observations was that managing the public sector properly was a major problem for democracies. He developed the idea that large businesses worked best when they were decentralised, rather than the command and control model (the Weberian idea of a bureaucracy). He also felt that highly centralised government programmes could not react quickly to changes. They needed "planned abandonment".

Businesses and governments have a tendency to cling to 'yesterday's successes' rather than seeing they are no longer useful.

Later in his life he became more aware of the importance of the 'third sector', the non profit- making organisation, neither privately nor government run – what we now call a 'social enterprise'. He argued that in a more complex society, organisations should be given objectives, and allowed to achieve them in their own way (Drucker, 1992; 2008[28]).

This new model of management with its focus on outcomes is underpinned by the drive for efficiency. Robert Peston[29] analyses what this means in practice. He describes the takeover of Travelodge by a venture capital company Permira. They sold off redundant assets and made money. They also introduced efficiency measures into the management of the hotels. The time taken to clean a room was reduced from 40 minutes to 25 minutes. This saved about £10 million per year. As a result, cleaners had to work harder and fewer were required. Their tasks were analysed and reorganised. Their pay did increase, but Permira was able to sell Travelodge to Dubai International Capital for a substantial profit. Travelodge became more efficient and did not go out of business. Whether the distribution of reward was fair as between the cleaners and the venture capitalists is another issue, and the public might not be happy if such a solution were applied to the NHS.

This approach has been largely criticised within the sociological literature. Richard Sennett has written about new forms of managerial organisations in two works, 'The Corrosion of Character' (1998) and 'The Culture of the New Capitalism' (2007). [30] He argues that although the old hierarchical bureaucracy which became the model for large corporations was "an iron cage", nevertheless workers were able to make sense of it and their place within an organisation (Sennett, 2007). A worker could gain seniority and status by working hard, and feel he or she had "achieved something". Sennett identified a sense of self-worth in public sector workers, who although badly paid, felt they were serving the public good. "The National Health Service ... gave them a positive, institutional place in British society" (Sennett,

2007). In the more disorganised post-Fordist society, however, these certainties are no more.

Sennett argues that the new "liquid modernity" (Sennett, 2007) does not necessarily bring more freedom as its apologists maintain. It is easier, with modern electronic communications, to maintain power from the centre. The system produces an apparent paradox – the concentration without the centralisation of power. This has been identified by Bennett Harrison (1994) in a study of modern corporations called 'Lean and Mean'.[31]

In the old-fashioned Weberian hierarchy, power came down a pyramid. People often 'mediated' or adapted instructions to suit their particular circumstances. Now it goes directly from the top to the front line.

Sennett dwells on the human consequences. People are displaced or transferred. Their record or seniority count for nothing.

## Changing the NHS management system

It would be helpful at this point to consider the views of post-Fordist theory and whether these are applicable to the NHS. The NHS was traditionally seen as a hierarchical organisation in the Weberian and Fordist mould.

> "The welfare state also assumed the form of a bureaucratic pyramid...The bureaucratic rules served the bureaucracy first and foremost; elderly, students, the unemployed, and the sick were obliged to behave like officeholders in the Weberian sense rather than as individuals with distinctive life histories. The system focussed ever more on institutional self-maintenance and stability rather than on the effective delivery of care."
>
> *(Sennett 2007)*

Many in the NHS might think Sennett's historical criticisms unfair, but there have been moves recently to make the service more flexible and responsive to patients (NHS Choices 2012[32]). More patient involvement is a consequence of this. Nevertheless, control, particularly over finance, is still in the hands of the centre.

Yet, it should be noted that the NHS is envied by many other countries which have private insurance systems either fully or in part. The NHS is much more able to keep costs under control than these systems are where the insurance companies and practitioners can charge higher prices (Bolton, 2004). The USA is perhaps the best example, but Germany, which has a system of state-sponsored health insurance, has now had to reduce the availability of some treatments.

Recent work on the NHS has looked at the change from a professionally-run NHS, where major decisions were left to the professionals, to a more market-orientated managerial system, where issues of financial accountability and measurement of effectiveness become more salient (Henderson, 2001; Klein, 2006[33]; Martin *et al.* 2010).

Particularly significant changes have included the imposition of new arrangements for financial accountability and the measurement of effectiveness; the 'marketisation' of structural arrangements between those who provide welfare services and those who pay for them; the marketisation of relations within service organisations; and attempts to change established relations between service providers and consumers (Exworthy and Halford, 1999[34]).

Commentators have given different explanations for the change. One is ideological – that during the 1980s, Thatcherite ideology deliberately sought to weaken the power of NHS professionals in order to favour private interests and reduce public spending on the NHS (Exworthy and Halford 1999; Klein 2006). In fact the Act which introduced the 'purchaser-provider' split was not introduced until 1990, in her eleventh year in government. [35]

Several commentators have commented that in fact NHS spending actually rose during this period (Hills, 1998). Private contractors did not play a major role in clinical services, and privatisation was mainly confined to catering, cleaning and laundry services (Exworthy and Halford, 1999; Klein, 2006). It was not until the New Labour era post-1997 that private contractors were able to provide some clinical services such as MRI scanning, and serious attempts are now being made to introduce the purchaser-provider split to services such as community health, which is noted in 'Our Care, Our Say' (DoH, 2006[36]). This meant that a Primary Care Trust would commission services from a separately managed and still publicly owned organisation managing areas such as nursing. This is now actually happening. In most cases Foundation Trusts have taken over community services, but in some cases they have become social enterprises, and there are now signs that private health firms may manage them. For example, outsourcing giant Serco has been selected as the preferred bidder for a three-year contract to provide community health services for NHS Suffolk worth £140 million (*Health Investor* magazine, March 22nd 2012[37]). There would then be scope to transfer these services to a privately managed body if the public one did not perform (Darzi, 2005 [38]). Such a model has already been applied to housing, where most repairs and maintenance services are now contracted out. Not all services would necessarily go to privately-run services. 'Our Care, Our Say' specifically refers to the expansion of 'third sector' organisations in health and social care services (DoH 2006).This refers to charities and other not for profit bodies.

What is happening in the NHS can best be described as what Handy calls a "task culture".[39] Put simply, this means that an organisation has to be flexible, and restructure itself to meet new challenges. This could be applied to integrating services at the front line. Professor Bob Hudson has studied examples of what this actually means. [40] Integrated networks can be made up of both private and public sectors.

## Public and patient involvement

How do these developments influence public and patient involvement? I shall consider this further in the next chapter, but if services are devolved to small locally based providers, this could give substantial opportunities for grass-roots involvement (Florin and Dixon, 2004[41]; Baggott, 2005[42]). If, on the other hand, healthcare is commissioned to large-scale private companies, the likelihood is that these will see patients as customers, and will value feedback from them as consumers of services. This will be in their interest if they wish to regain contracts, but is unlikely to afford local people much direct influence on how the service is provided (Hudson, 2007; Baggott, 2005).

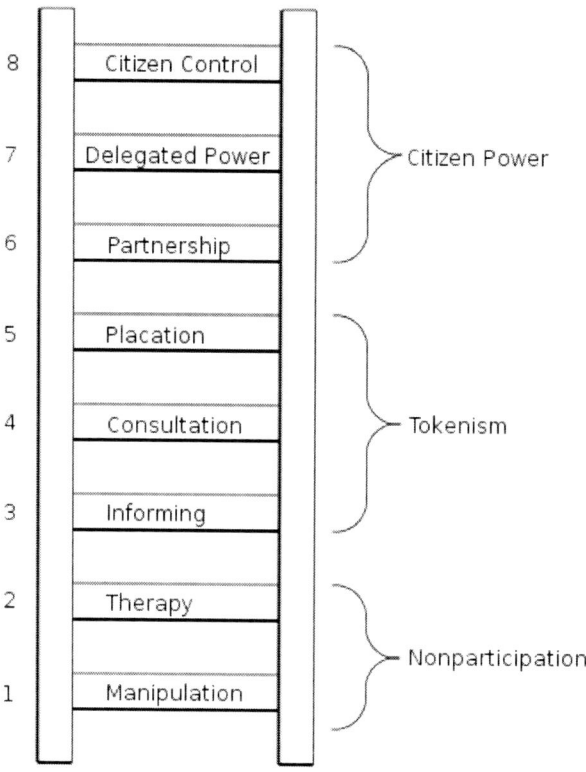

Does involvement by the public and patients have any place in these models? The classic work of Sherry Arnstein provides a way of measuring success. Arnstein investigated the citizen involvement programmes which were set up as part of the 'Great Society' welfare programme organised by the Johnson administration in the US in the 1960s. In 1969 she constructed 'A Ladder of Citizen Participation' (Arnstein, 1969: 216-224)[43]). It has degrees of participation, in the manner of a Weberian continuum. The ladder shows a progression from 'non-participation' to 'tokenism' to actual 'citizen power, and is a useful tool for identifying actual practice. An issue with this schema, however, is that the terms used may carry moral overtones. 'Manipulation' has connotations of deviousness, and 'tokenism' of deception, whereas 'citizen control' would appeal to left-wing thinkers, but perhaps not some others.

Whether participation is judged as successful depends on what it sets out to do in the first place, and 'citizen control' might not be desirable in clinical matters. In the health context, for example, citizen control might be the objective for a particular project, such as improvements in a particular cancer treatment, but not for the overall direction of regional health policy. Commissioning, as distinct from provision of services, will continue to be managed publicly; at the time of writing this is by the new clinical commissioning groups, although future arrangements are uncertain. It would be their responsibility to ensure proper public involvement.

Again, they could see it as a way of ensuring customer feedback, so as to better monitor their contractors, as distinct from a strong public voice in how services are provided (Florin and Dixon, 2004; Baggott, 2005).

## Integrated working styles

Research in the North East, conducted by Bob Hudson, was developed in order to understand the practical consequences of these models with reference to the devolved and integrated styles of working in the NHS. As noted above this approach is recommended in 'Our Care, Our Say' (DoH, 2006; Hudson, 2006[44]; 2008[45]). He completed a study of integrated team working in the Sedgefield area of Durham in 2006. This looked at a project involving Sedgefield Primary Care Trust, Sedgefield Borough Council and Durham County Council. These three partners established five locality-based teams, collocated from line teams across the borough, each consisting of social workers, district nurses and housing officers. This project is a practical example of devolution down to a non-hierarchical team. The project meant professional boundaries and hierarchies were broken down. Hudson (2006) notes that it had the effect of producing faster responses, since people talked to each other rather than going through lengthy procedures. Greater trust also developed between different professionals. Hudson does note, however, that there were organisational and professional barriers to be overcome as well as ominously described "political dilemmas". What is important is that the project delivered on the ground.

Easington PBC Board is currently considering two Integrated Care Initiatives in the Easington area for mental health and long-term conditions. The draft scoping documents have were prepared in January 2010, and feature in the empirical work of this study. (Durham PCT, 2010) Although the practical details of implementation have been highlighted during the consultation, it is too early to comment yet on their practical consequences. In a paper produced by the Care Services Improvement Partnership (2004) Bob Hudson looks at some of the theoretical issues of 'whole systems working (Hudson, 2004). He notes that practitioners have identified what they call "wicked issues". These are problems which are hard to identify but also do not fall under the jurisdiction of any one agency or department. Health inequality is often described as such an issue. Anti-social behaviour is another. Such issues require integrated working (Hudson, 2006)

The Community Services White Paper of January 2006 talks of the need to encourage all health partners to work together in a system-wide approach to developing urgent care services, including better care for patients with long-term conditions, shifting care from acute hospitals to the community, promoting better public health, integration with social care and improving access to GPs. (DoH, 2006, p90)

This is an example of 'inter-agency working', or 'whole systems' as Hudson prefers to call it. It is not always easy to work in such an unpredictable and changing climate. Complexity theorists talk of 'complex adaptive systems'. Langton (1990) describes this as the "edge of chaos". [46] Hudson describes this as "a zone wherein uncertainty and insufficient agreement can obscure the choice of next step, though there is not so much disagreement and uncertainty that the system is thrown into chaos".

Chaos theory can be useful in considering current developments in the NHS. As Hudson (2004) points out, the emphasis is now on shifting resources from the acute sector to the community, whereas at the same time Acute Trusts have tied themselves into PFI deals. This could mean still paying for a hospital which is no longer used or even demolished.

However, the concept of services being focused on the patient or client rather than simply being managed in a top-down way does emphasise the importance of patient and public involvement (Hudson, 2005). The reaction of patients and other stakeholders will be one of the main judges of success of programmes if traditional performance evaluation mechanisms are less easy to implement in a joined up system (Hudson, 2005). Resulting from this work we can see an NHS where there is more emphasis on integrated working with other agencies (some of which may be third or private sector). At the same time there is considerable attention to achieving value for money as more demands are put onto already squeezed budgets, with people living longer and equipment and drugs costing more. Thus, effective measurement of outputs and performance is now given high priority, and this is one objective behind the reforms which have recently become law. The idea of actually putting services out to tender, or considering it as a veiled threat to improve performance, is here to stay, as are the consequences of adopting techniques of the private sector to improve efficiency within the NHS (Cooper, et al, 2010 [47]).It is rumoured that one PCT even considered using management techniques from the car industry to improve performance. Back to Fordism!

## Conflict of control and devolution

The brief survey of the literature indicates a real tension at the heart of the NHS. The demands on the system are increasing all the time, yet funding is constrained. At the moment, the system commands widespread public support, and it is in the interests of the government to ensure that this remains, particularly if additional resources are required from the taxpayer to finance it. The government wants to keep tight control of the finances and control costs. It only has to look across the Atlantic to see what happens where there is not this control. At the same time, however, it is widely recognised that if health is to improve, particularly as people live longer, it is essential that more resources are devoted to health promotion and the prevention of disease rather than simply acute provision. This will mean more flexible working and integrated working with other agencies. It will also mean involving the public, particularly with long-term care and health promotion. More flexibility means more devolution to local services.

One of the concerns many people have with the new Health and Social Care Act is that privatisation of services will disrupt these networks. Commercial firms may not wish to disclose data to other organisations, or may regard them as competitors. If health is treated as a consumable 'product' they will not see any reason for involving people, or listening to their ideas, other than as a form of market research.

The NHS seems sincere about its desire to involve patients and the public, and also remarkably candid about its shortcomings in the past. The conflict seems to be between the need for control, particularly of finance, and the need at the same time to devolve power downwards to the local level. The NHS frequently states that an aim of involvement is improvement, and the patients and the public will only judge such work a success if they can see visible signs of improvement as a result of their efforts. As Darzi notes, they may not think withdrawing or reorganising a particular service as an 'improvement'. Proper involvement requires a dialogue and considerable effort. In the next chapter, I shall look more closely at the mechanisms for involvement within the NHS, and how effective and useful they are.

*This chapter finds that the original challenges facing the NHS were restoring hospitals and dealing with epidemics. The challenges today are more likely to be diseases concerned with unhealthy lifestyles or conditions associated with old age. Management is now much more devolved to individual units away from the traditional hierarchical structure, a tendency which is apparent in other large organisations. In an attempt to ensure value for money and contain costs, units are expected to work on commercial lines, and although management may be devolved, finances are strictly controlled. Many see this as a strength of the NHS.*

*There have been attempts to work with other agencies in a more flexible way, and it seems that such an approach will be necessary to deal with the challenges facing the NHS now. The wider community will also have to be involved..*

*There is a tension between the desire to move more resources into the community, and the acute services which wish to retain facilities and prestige. There are also concerns about how the privatisation of services could prevent networking between different agencies.*

# CHAPTER 4

# PATIENT AND PUBLIC
# INVOLVEMENT: AN OVERVIEW

*This chapter looks at the development of mechanisms for involvement by patients and the public in the NHS. Various initiatives have been tried and replaced. The position now is somewhat confusing. The introduction of practice-based commissioning gave a new importance to involvement, but what its objectives actually are is often unclear, although it is usually thought of as desirable. An attempt is made to define them.*

## The development of PPI

INVOLVEMENT IN various forms had been developing since 1974. As I have indicated in Chapter 3, it was not seen as a major issue before then. The establishment of the Community Health Councils was a reaction to the fact that some services were transferred from local authority to NHS control. These were intended to represent the public interest and included councillors (Timmins, 1995).They were funded by the Department of Health and were accessible to the public, often with offices in town centres and a permanent member of staff to organise them and ensure decisions were implemented. The CHCs were able to investigate complaints and refer them to the hospitals' complaints procedures. They were also able to investigate issues and challenge the hospital authorities (Levitt, 1980).[48]

The performance of the CHCs varied, but they continued until the 2001 Health and Social Care Act and the establishment of the Commission for Patient and Public Involvement in Health (CPPIH) in January 2003. Many hospitals had also established patients' councils to advise them on their concerns. These groups would often also contain ex-patients and members of the public who had an association with the hospital (HSCA, 2001; Kennedy, 2001). There were also groups of hospital volunteers and friends who raised funds for improvements.

Yet, failure of the system was highlighted by the Kennedy Report of 2001[49] into events at Bristol Royal Infirmary after the deaths of children receiving cardiac surgical services at the hospital between 1984 and 1995. Its conclusions about public involvement and the attitudes of some professionals to the public were very forceful:

> "The result, however, has not been a sense of growing empowerment, such that the public, as patients or as taxpayers, after all these years of supposed involvement, feel truly in partnership with the professionals who run and provide our healthcare service. Indeed, the evidence from Bristol is the opposite: a sense, among many parents, of disempowerment, of inability to get the healthcare service to address their needs, and of bewilderment about where or to whom they could turn for help."
>
> *(Kennedy, 2001)*

In evidence to the enquiry, the NHS Primary Care Group Alliance wrote:

> "Being sincere about involving patients and the public in making decisions about their own care or about local health services involves a shift of power. Until individuals working in the NHS are ready for that, any user or public involvement in decision making will be a token event."
>
> *(BRI Inquiry, 2001)*

Following the 2001 Social Care Act a complex structure of PPI was created. Local authorities were given greater power of scrutiny and set up Overview and Scrutiny Committees. An independent complaints system was established (ICAS), and the Commission for Patient and Public Involvement (CPPIH) set up. This set up patients' forums which replaced the old, much loved Community Health Councils. CPPIH was later replaced by LINks (Local Involvement Networks) in 2008, and these appear to now be on the point of being reorganised into Healthwatch (2012).

So a complex structure of PPI has been created, with each part playing a different role. Things were complicated by the fact that individual trusts also made their own arrangements. Mari Robbins sets out the complicated structure in the classic Medical Secretaries' Handbook (2006). [50]

CPPIH achieved some success, particularly its investigation into dentistry [51], but the general feeling was that involvement mechanisms were both too complicated and ineffective.

The 2006 Health Act laid a duty on NHS organisations to involve users (section 242). In 2008 the NHS Constitution was published. This sets out the provisions of the 2006 Act. This guarantees public involvement in the NHS as follows:

> "You have the right to be involved in discussions and decisions about your healthcare, and to be given information to enable you to do this ... ".
>
> *(DoH 2008b, Section 2a).*

The main development in recent years has been the development of practice-based commissioning since 2006. This emphasises public engagement (see below).

Many volunteers involved in the NHS still feel that the CHCs were the best system. This continues to exist in Wales and Scotland (Board of Community Health Councils, Wales 2010; Community Health Partnerships, Scottish Executive, 2004[52]). The main complaint of those involved in the system is the constant reorganisation. Healthwatch is now being established to replace LINks.[53] All this seems to indicate that the Department of Health does not seem to be able to find an effective way of making involvement work.

The Overview and Scrutiny Committees have developed their expertise and have done some good work, but their future is now problematic with the new reforms. The government proposes Health and Wellbeing Boards to link local authorities with the NHS. How these will work has yet to be seen. Their possible development is considered further in Chapter Eight.

## Practice-based commissioning

Perhaps the most promising development is practice-based commissioning (PBC), which was introduced in the white paper 'Our Care, Our Say' in 2006. It is of considerable importance, both as a new way of involving people and as the underlying idea behind the 2012 Health and Social Care Bill. PBC is where a group of GPs and other health professionals can put proposals for new community-based services to the local PCT. If the PCT approves it will fund the ventures (DoH, 2008b).

The NHS defines the process as follows:

> "Commissioning in the NHS is the process of ensuring that the health and care services provided effectively meet the needs of the population... It is a complex process with responsibilities ranging from assessing population needs, prioritising health outcomes, procuring products and services, and managing service providers."
>
> *(DoH, 2009)*

The aim is to move services out of hospitals into the community wherever possible. Power shifts from the Acute Trusts to the people on the ground, the GPs.

The official guidance states:

> "Practice-based commissioning will lead to high quality services for patients in local and convenient settings. GPs, nurses and other primary care professionals are in the prime position to translate patient needs into redesigned services that best deliver what local people want."

(DoH, 2009)

In other words, it represents what is needed/wanted at a grass-roots level. Detailed guidance to GPs published in 2006 states proposals will only be considered if a business case is established. The criteria for assessing business cases will include:

> "Whether there has been proper involvement of patients and the public, particularly what are known as 'hard to reach groups'."

(DoH, 2006)

## GP incentives for public consultation

Thus there is an incentive, if PBC is to work, for GPs to have evidence that they have consulted the public. A document published by the Department of Health in June 2009 identifies good practice, including an example of how COPD services were redesigned locally in Easington. These are all examples of where GPs have organised projects in the community and drawn down, or 'unbundled' funds from the PCT to do so (DoH, 2006).

Examples given include:

- The COPD project in Easington which helps patients to 'self-manage' the condition and thus avoid unnecessary trips to hospital;

- A community palliative care service which allows patients to stay in their own homes rather than be admitted to hospital in Bournemouth and Poole;

- A community glaucoma service in Liverpool.

The objective is to enable patients to access treatment and support where possible in the community. This is particularly attractive in areas which are not near acute hospitals. As noted above more sophisticated methods and higher standards inevitably seem to lead to fewer specialist acute hospitals, and the converse of this is that hopefully people visit them less frequently but access more services locally (Robbins, 2006). This is sometimes a difficult concept to explain to patients who have been used to visiting a local hospital.

There is now an incentive for GPs to involve the public, particularly 'hard to reach' groups, if they wish to engage in PBC. Arrangements have to be made to show this is being done. Now that the 2012 Act has been passed Clinical Commissioning groups are being established to take on the responsibility of commissioning healthcare from the PCTs which will disappear in 2013.

In fact most of the ideas which have been developed in the 2012 Act can be seen in 'Our Care, Our Say' published in January 2006. There is a substantial section on local involvement:

> "At the same time as giving people greater choice and control over the services they use, there is also a need to ensure that everyone in society has a voice that is heard. When people get involved and use their voice they can shape improvements in provision and contribute to greater fairness in service use."
>
> *(DoH, 2006, para 7.4)*

> "There is progress that we can build on. Some organisations in the NHS, local government and the voluntary, community and private sectors have engaged users and citizens in a systematic and robust way. However, these are not the norm. We want to see all parts of health and social care open and responsive to what people feel and prefer."
>
> *(DoH, 2006, para 7.7)*

> "Commissioning is the process whereby public resources are used effectively to meet the needs of local people. The voices of local people will be vitally important in improving this process. Public involvement is part of our wider strategy to facilitate high-quality commissioning and, in particular, to make joint commissioning a reality."
>
> *(DoH, 2006)*

I am deliberately giving considerable attention to PBC. It is fairly obvious that the origins of the present bill lie in the 2006 document 'Our Care, Our Say'. Although the original proposals were to allow "different providers to compete for services", the then Labour government restricted involvement by the private sector to 15% of NHS activity. It also did not abolish PCTs, but encouraged them to work with PBC groups. As a result, Cumbria PCT handed its budget over to the new groups, and other authorities such as Northamptonshire worked closely with them. Other PCTs, like Durham, were less willing to do so. PCTs were also encouraged to do joint commissioning with social services, and in some areas, such as Northumberland, joint health and social care trusts were established.

## Public involvement as a measure of performance management

It is interesting to note how public involvement is seen as a measure of performance management. The NHS sets out its ideas about involvement in the document 'Real Involvement' (2008), which is a guide to how NHS organisations should implement section 242 of the 2006 Act. The Principles of Local Accountability and Involvement are set out in Part 1, Section 2. NHS involvement practices should be:

1. Clear;
2. Accessible and transparent;
3. Open;
4. Inclusive;
5. Responsive;
6. Sustainable;
7. Proactive;
8. Focused on improvement.

    (DoH 2008)

The last three items are perhaps those that merit further investigation. One would expect all public bodies to observe the first four (whether they actually do is another debate!). However, the NHS is aiming to establish long-term relationships with the community which will build trust, and not simply consult people when a proposal has been made. Instead it wishes to engage in a dialogue with people, seeking to explain why changes are necessary rather than simply announcing they will happen. The NHS appears to be aware it has 'previous'. Past practice has often presented the public with what appears to be a fait accompli, a proposal with no other alternative on a 'take it or leave it' basis (DoH, 2008). This has bred distrust of the whole process amongst the public, and the NHS appears to recognise this. In fact, the introduction to the publication is remarkably candid:

> "While nationally there are many examples of innovative practice, there is still little evidence that involvement is a mainstream activity alongside other policy and performance requirements ... There is scant evidence to show that involvement activity is stitched into all the strands of NHS organisations' work ....We also know that the NHS is not always sure about when it needs to involve users and clear about whether involving users is the same or different to consulting them."
>
> *(DoH, 2008: 10)*

Public involvement is mentioned as being particularly important as part of commissioning. The main reason for involvement from the NHS's perspective, is set out as point 7, "Focused on Improvement". This is not always clear as far as the public is concerned. The loss of an old and much loved institution does not always appear as an improvement. Lord Darzi commented in his interim report in 2007 (54) that:

> "We need to reassure patients and the public that change is necessary and that it will improve the care they receive ... We should be clear from the outset that no major service change should happen except on the basis of need and sound clinical evidence. ... and that consultation should proceed only where there is effective and early engagement with the public, clear evidence of improved outcomes for patients, and resources available to enable new facilities to open alongside old ones closing."
>
> *(Darzi, 2008)*

The consultations which generate the most noise and are often the most contentious are those to reconfigure services. The public does not always understand clinical issues. They are usually far more concerned about access and the loss of status for a particular town if it no longer has a hospital. Consultation needs explanation and dialogue (Darzi, 2008). Nevertheless, it is still essentially a reactive process, as distinct from the planning of future provision. In Part 1, Section 4 of 'Real Involvement' the report sets out the principles of involvement in commissioning. As described earlier, commissioning is about planning future NHS activity, and also evaluating what is most effective. Thus the Report acknowledges:

> "User involvement in the commissioning process is not well established and presently it is more likely to occur in designing services than in assessing needs or evaluating services. For example, one or two user representatives may attend a commissioning meeting, but there are many other decisions that precede or follow this stage. Much more thought needs to be given as to how best to involve users throughout the commissioning cycle."
>
> *(DoH, 2008: Section 4, p.96)*

This is perhaps the part of PPI which is least well developed. It is means planning what the NHS should do in the future, rather than reacting to what it is doing now.

# Conclusion

At the end of the first decade of the new century, and almost ten years after the passing of the 2001 Act, a complex system of public and patient involvement is now in place. This study does not seek to compare the different avenues to participation. They have different emphases and purposes, and arrangements are different in various parts of the country. As indicated, new developments in PBC require local involvement. It is unclear as yet how effective this is.

Four broad aims from involvement can be identified from the different approached which have been described above:

- *Scrutiny:* The work of the OSCs and LINks, which feeds into the OSCs. These bodies consider and if necessary criticise the activities of the NHS. By law the NHS must respond.

- *Partnership:* Carers, patients and other interested parties work with the NHS to improve services. There are often groups to consider particular illnesses or conditions. Within this category can be placed individuals who are now taking a greater role to manage their own treatment or care, particularly those with long-term conditions.

- *Forward planning:* The commissioning role which considers future planning. This is a role at present for the PCTs, but will now pass to the new clinical commissioning groups (CCGs).

- *Customer feedback:* With the increasing complexity and variety of NHS provision, those who commission care want to know whether that care is working and what improvements can be made. PPI has a role here.

It is understandable that PPI arrangements will evolve as the NHS develops and changes, but the frequent changes of recent years appear to be an admission that the process is not yet deemed to be right. A positive sign, however, lies in the provisions in the 2012 Act for greater involvement in health by local government, through the Health and Wellbeing boards and the direct management of public health. This will be given more consideration in a later chapter.

There is great emphasis on involvement in both the original 2006 proposals for PBC and in the 2012 Act which has now abolished PCTs and handed commissioning over to the clinical groups. There will still be a 'commissioning organisation' which will organise things for the commissioning groups. This could consist of ex-PCT staff, or could be a private organisation. To what extent it will organise public engagement will depend on whether the new clinical commissioning groups decide to pay for it. The debate is ongoing, but a strong body of opinion, including the BMA, would like the engagement arrangements for the CCGs to be 'in-house' and there does seem to be a logic in that if public engagement is going to influence commissioning decisions.

The other important point, which I am sure is fairly obvious, is that the ideas produced by Andrew Lansley did not appear from outer space. They were already well established within the NHS, and it seems that public engagement should have a major role within the new commissioning groups. A future government will have a situation where this system is in place and the challenge will be to make it work in line with the basic principles I have outlined at the beginning of this book. It is unlikely anyone will want to resurrect the PCTs!

---

*There are various strands to involvement, and four objectives have been defined:*

- *Scrutiny – largely done by local authorities;*

- ***Partnership working*** *– schemes to discourage unhealthy lifestyles and to care for those with long-term conditions;*

- ***Forward planning*** *– to involve the public in the planning of services;*

- ***Customer feedback*** *–to see how effective services are.*

*The introduction of PBC commissioning will certainly empha-sise the last two objectives. Closer working with local government could also increase public involvement. The fact that various different initiatives have been tried and then reorganised seems to be an admission that the NHS has not yet got involvement right.*

---

# CHAPTER 5

# INVOLVEMENT AT A LOCAL LEVEL

*This chapter looks at local examples of involvement in the Easington area and considers how valuable they are, and in particular whether they make health services more accountable to the local community. There are many schemes, and this does not purport to be a representative or comprehensive sample, just examples I have encountered. Nevertheless, they show different aspects of what successful involvement can achieve.*

As I HAVE described above, there is much talk about 'involvement' and 'accountability' in the literature about the NHS without much actual investigation as to whether these terms actually mean anything, and how important are they to ordinary people. More importantly, what is actually being done at grassroots level which means anything to ordinary people? The effectiveness or otherwise of measures to ensure involvement and accountability also has an important impact as to whether services should be publicly or privately provided.

Involvement has been discussed in the previous chapter, but accountability needs to be properly defined. It means that individuals and organisations should be held to account for what they do, both in the private and public sectors. For this to be effective, there needs to be transparency, which means that information is made available to a wider public. Organisations need to have some form of governance, which means independent people, whether elected or appointed, oversee what is going on. This body must make sure that proper procedures are followed, and the organisation is doing what it is supposed to do, whether the directions come from the public, their representatives, or shareholders.

Involvement of both the public and clients is a way of enhancing accountability in the public sector. In the private sector, success is often measured in whether an organisation makes a profit, but this is not usually a criterion in the public sector. Feedback from patients and the public can give some idea of whether bodies are performing properly and achieving their proper objectives. So involvement is a necessary condition for proper accountability, as well as the other reasons which have been discussed in detail in the previous chapter.

There are many examples from both the public and the private sector which show how there can be abuses when there are not proper systems of accountability. Overspending on defence contracts, waste on NHS computer systems which do not work, News International, Nigerian oil exploration, banks which speculate too riskily, and so on.

## Involvement schemes in practice

First I shall look at the various involvement schemes currently operating in the district of Easington, County Durham and assess whether they improve services and provide some sort of accountability to the local population.

### Easington's characteristics

Easington was a separate local government district until 2009, when it was merged into the unitary county of Durham. It contains two towns (Peterlee and Seaham), both with populations of over 20,000, and several large industrial ex-coalmining villages. Communications within the district have always been poor, and the villages maintained a fierce sense of independence. The area is still referred to as Easington, and is treated as an NHS 'locality'.

The badge of the old District of Easington Council included a miners' lamp, a wheat sheaf and a ship to symbolise the three main characteristics of the area, mining, agriculture and seafaring (Seaham is the only port in County Durham). In 1980 mining was still the dominant industry, employing over 10,000 men. 1,400 people were still employed in the industry in 1993 when the last pit, Easington Colliery, closed (DETR, 1998;[55] Smith, 2010[56]). Since then there have been various attempts to bring new industry into the area. Much regeneration money has been spent in the villages and Seaham, and a major boost was when the housing provider, East Durham Homes, achieved government funding to regenerate the housing stock.(CLG Committee, 2010[57]).

The decline of the coal industry was a severe blow to the district. A raft of statistics in the 1980s and 1990s indicated problems in all areas. Educational achievement was lower than both the average for the country and the county of Durham. In recent years, rates of educational achievement have improved, and the latest figures (2004) show that the Easington area is no longer the worst in the county. Economic inactivity, including sickness and early retirement, peaked at 25% at the turn of the century, although the figure has fallen somewhat now.

Townsend's report on health and deprivation in 1987 cited Wheatley Hill as the unhealthiest ward in England (Townsend et al, 1987; Phillimore and Beattie, 1994[58]). Deaths from circulatory disease, cancer and respiratory disease are higher than the national average, as are rates for smoking, obesity and teenage pregnancies. Easington also vied with Hull for the title of 'obesity capital' of the country. Premature death rates and the high numbers of people with limiting long-term illnesses completed a gloomy picture (Walker, 2009[59]).

Historically, it could be suggested that the Easington area has been traditionally isolated and, from a health point of view, neglected. One of the reasons was that it was on the edge of the catchment area of three hospitals, Hartlepool, Durham and Sunderland, and suffered as a result.

## Easington involvement initiatives

The establishment of a separate PCT for the Easington area in 2002 led to considerable improvements. The PCT was able to lobby, together with the local authority, for more resources, and met with some success. The Easington PCT worked with the District Council to run a large scale public involvement programme. The Easington PCT was merged into the larger County Durham PCT in 2006. This was followed by the District Council being reformed into the new unitary authority of County Durham in 2009. Many people appear to look back to the period when Easington had its own PCT and District Council as a golden age for public and patient involvement.

The White Paper, "Our Care, Our Say" was published in 2006, and advocated the formation of local boards of GPs to put proposals for commissioning services to their local PCT. As part of the process they were obliged to consult patients and the public. Easington PCT established a Practice Based Commissioning Board of the local GPs in 2006, and this group established a 'Shadow Board' consisting of representatives of GP forums and local community groups to advise the GPs on commissioning priorities. This group changed its name to Monitoring and Advisory Board (MAB) in 2009.

The new county-wide PCT did not put the resources into public engagement that the previous Easington PCT had. To be fair the County Overview and Scrutiny Committee (OSC) developed its expertise and became more effective, working with the LINks network. Activities tended to be more centred on Durham City, and many people saw the Easington MAB as the main vehicle for public engagement in the area.

In 2010 I undertook some research with Dr Stephen MacDonald from Sunderland University about public engagement in the Easington NHS area. We targeted the role and effectiveness of the Monitoring and Advisory Board ('The Role of Public and Patient involvement in Practice Based Commissioning within Easington NHS Services', MacDonald and Taylor-Gooby, July 2010[60]).

The research involved interviewing ordinary patients, lay members of the MAB and GPs. The results were very clear. The enthusiasm and commitment of all those concerned was very apparent and in many ways humbling. There is a reservoir of voluntary effort and commitment which the NHS can tap into. People want to volunteer, and want to feel that they contribute to the NHS. But they also want to be taken seriously, and feel that what they are doing is having some effect. If they feel that their involvement is tokenistic and being organised simply so that the NHS can claim it is involving people, they will not want to continue.

What the study indicated was that there is enthusiasm to make PBC work through involvement at a local level, although at present there are barriers, mainly financial.

When the study was done in 2010, the PCT appeared reluctant to delegate commissioning decisions, although the proposals in the new Health and Social Care Act 2012 lwill require them to do so. How this works will be interesting and may merit further research.

Some volunteers may simply wish to improve the way their local GP surgery is run, or have a say in how health facilities are organised in their particular village or community. It was clear that the Health Forums which had been organised by the old Easington PCT with small delegated budgets, where there was an effective chair, could bring substantial benefits to their particular areas, particularly if they worked with other bodies such as parish councils. The funding was withdrawn in 2011, which I feel was a retrograde step as far as involvement is concerned. The role of the Forums will be further explained below.

Some GP practices also have Patients' Groups. Others do not, and there is no clear evidence as to why this is, but if the NHS wants to encourage involvement at a grassroots level then it needs to pursue a policy of encouraging them to be established (possibly by offering administrative support). At the time of writing, the new commissioning group is encouraging their establishment. Information supplied by County Durham LINks (Co Durham LINks 2010) indicates that GP Practice Groups are functioning for about half the GP practices in the county.

I spoke to a senior manager at the PCT who explained that there were extensive mechanisms for involvement in the NHS.

What she meant was that there were mechanisms for surveys where people could express their views, and that is undoubtedly true.

## Provision of services at the local level

However, the people we interviewed did not seem very interested in things like that. They all wanted to be involved in the provision of services at a local level. Some wanted to improve the service at their local surgery. Others were involved where the focus was on dealing with patients with long-term conditions, and programmes to prevent people having to go to hospital such as COPD. There was also a willingness to become involved in projects promoting healthy lifestyles, such as weight management and alcohol.

The local professionals interviewed wanted to develop more community-based projects, aimed at providing community treatment, such as weight management and diabetes, but felt they were not getting access to the necessary funding. These projects could involve community volunteers in a social marketing role, publicising what was happening and encouraging people to take part. The volunteers all wanted active involvement in the improvement of services. They did not seem very interested in survey work, or developing policy.

The MAB organised seminars to consider its wider commissioning role, such as to which acute trusts patients should be sent. This involved discussion between GPs, consultants and lay representatives. This was a radical departure, but not the form of involvement most people wanted. As indicated above, they wanted something to do with their local NHS.

The survey did produce evidence that PBC can mobilise local people, patients and voluntary organisations to work in partnership with GPs and other health professionals to deliver a better NHS locally, with the emphasis on promoting better health and preventing illness. Some treatments could be taken out of hospitals and delivered in the community. Examples would be 'stop smoking' or 'weight management' programmes, or diabetes and COPD clinics. Health professionals provide the expertise necessary, but local people and organisations can publicise the schemes and involve the people who need to be reached.

It is often observed that the hospitals in the North East are of a high standard, but health is poor compared to the rest of the UK. One way to help reduce these health inequalities are the sort of community-based projects to promote better health with which the MAB has been involved .This will require more funding at a local level. People spoke with enthusiasm of the various arrangements of the old PCT and District Council where they actually had influence over how resources were spent locally. Having this influence encourages and mobilises volunteers.

It will be interesting to see whether the new Health and Social Care Act does have the effect of bringing resources down nearer to the community.

## Health Forums

Mention has already been made of 'Health Forums' and I alluded to the one in Blackhall in the introduction. The term needs to be more fully explained. GP practices organise groups of patients to offer suggestions for improvements, and these are sometimes referred to as 'forums', but to avoid confusion I have called them 'patients' groups'. The Forums referred to are bodies originally established by the Easington PCT in all the main settlements in the Easington area. These bodies consisted of local stakeholders, and worked with local councils and other community bodies. (The old District of Easington was totally 'parished', that is, covered by lower-tier local authorities called parish councils, or in the case of Peterlee and Seaham, Town Councils. Each Health Forum had a small budget and professional help to organise the meetings, take minutes etc. The Forums organised projects to improve health locally, and were able to use their modest funding to draw down other funding.

When the Easington PCT was abolished in 2006 the new County Durham PCT took on the organisation of the Forums, but resources were now less than they had been. Many of them ceased to function, but several persisted, notably in Horden and Blackhall. The PCT finally withdrew the funding in 2011, leaving the remaining forums to manage as best they could. I visited a meeting of the Blackhall one to see what they were doing.

In the past it has supported various schemes, including a project to install low-level lighting in senior citizens' homes to minimise the risk of falls, outdoor ventures for the cadets and other youth groups, and an allotment. The actual spending of the money was properly monitored.

The group no longer receives PCT funding as the PCT has had to reduce spending by 30% under the QIPP programme (Quality, Innovation, Productivity and Prevention – a programme to secure better value for money) but the local county councillor has given it some funding from his own budget to allow it to continue. The meeting received an application from a youth group while I was there.

What impressed me was their enthusiasm and determination to keep going. An example of how they could mobilise volunteers was a 'broth day' at the community centre where senior citizens came in for their broth and received their flu jab at the same time. Not very glamorous, but contributing to local health.

## The Hospital of God, Greatham – a third sector organisation

Through the Blackhall Health Forum I was put in contact with another body which operates in the Easington area – the Hospital of God at Greatham. This is an interesting organisation – iit dates back to the eleventh century and originally provided almshouses for the poor, funded by the Diocese of Durham. I talked to some of the staff and the following points came up:

- As a third sector organisation with extensive activities in the east of Durham, the Hospital of God provides better value for money with services than some statutory organisations.

- Some guests are part-funded by social services. This funding is becoming more restricted. As a result some families are choosing to fund their relative privately, and some are at risk of dropping out completely.

- The organisation provides support for carers and is in the process of introducing an evening service.

- There appears to be poor communication with social services on some occasions.

- There is an active group of carers who help organise events and give their advice/suggestions to the management.

- The discussion also covered wider issues about the role of the voluntary sector and the future direction of the NHS. There is a need for integrated working between the NHS/social services and the third sector. The third sector can save the NHS money by providing support when people are discharged from hospital, thus preventing them being readmitted. The hospitals are under pressure to discharge people because of their performance indicators. The third sector can be more innovative and flexible, and harness community resources more.

- We also discussed the Blackhall Health Forum, which was very good at spreading awareness in the wider community.

It is certainly true that the Hospital of God has innovated and its services are very popular. Reductions in social care funding appear to be restricting some of its activities, and the frequent complaint of lack of communication with social services does give cause for concern. Organisations like the Hospital of God have considerable resources, and working in partnership with the NHS and social services does appear beneficial to all. The organisation also appears to be good at mobilising volunteers. As a charity, it has a board of trustees which is required to publish accounts.

## Healthworks

So far I have looked at the attitudes of people involved with the commissioning process, the Blackhall Health Forum, and a charity. I now need to consider the other big legacy of the old PCT in the Easington area – Healthworks.

Healthworks is in Easington Colliery. [62] The establishment of Healthworks was the result of an initiative from the Horden and Easington Neighbourhood Pathfinder (additional funding directed at coalfield areas by the 1997 Labour government), the local authority, and the local primary care trust (Easington PCT). The aim was to bring various service providers together in one venue and provide a Healthy Living Resource Centre. There was a widespread consultation involving 4,000 homes and at least four large community engagement events.

The centre, formally the old waterworks building, opened in 2007. The actual building was gifted from Northumbria Water for 25 years. When the service began in 2007, 11 services were on offer and seven partners involved. A year later, the GP walk-in service was introduced, available from 8am to 8pm seven days per week. Now there are more than 70 services/activities and partners involved.

The provider of the service is now County Durham and Darlington NHS Foundation Trust, which has recently taken over community services, and the centre forms part of their Health Improvement Service. (For those not familiar with the sometimes arcane workings of the NHS, the Durham Foundation Trust (FT) which runs the main hospital in Durham, also manages the community services which were originally managed by the PCT on their behalf. The implications of this 'integrated pathway' will be explored in the next chapter). There is a strong steering group which sets the overall direction of the centre and monitors its impact. There is another group of tenants and service providers which initiates partnership working, information sharing and help to avoid duplication of services. Healthworks liaises with other organisations in the area such as the Welfare Hall (previously the miners' hall, now a community centre.) An example of joint working is the 'fit communities consortium' which involves 14 community centres throughout East Durham and aims to increase physical activity opportunities for all. The Healthworks coordinator chairs the group and the other centres are actively involved in agreeing a joint action plan, securing funding and consultation.

What is unique about the centre is its level of community engagement and its responsiveness to community needs. This can be demonstrated in its vibrant volunteer programme and its range of services. At present, 60 volunteers are involved with the centre and they are a valuable asset to a small workforce of five paid staff. Volunteers can gain qualifications, experience and confidence whilst still being able to claim benefits; this in turn increases their employability.

I visited one of the groups which uses the centre, the MS Support Group. It raises its own funding, but secretarial support and accommodation are supplied by Healthworks. The group told me how important mutual support and encouragement were. MS is an unpredictable condition. A victim can be fine one day, and then very tired the next. People who were fit and active feel very embarrassed about using a wheelchair. At Healthworks, they have their own keep-fit worker and organise excursions and other activities. Specialised gym equipment is very expensive, but the group hopes to obtain funding as an independent body. The whole point of the group is to sustain and encourage the sufferers so they can lead as normal lives as possible.

## Durham Deafened Support

This brief snapshot tries to capture some of the diverse range of voluntary and community activity taking place in the Easington area and aligned to the NHS. Before concluding I want to mention one more voluntary body (or social enterprise if you prefer the term) – Durham Deafened Support.

This was begun in 1998 by Jane Atkinson, who set out to close a huge gap in the system after losing her hearing and finding she didn't fit in. She was English speaking, a non-BSL (British Sign Language) user and did not use hearing aids or amplified phones etc. She described herself as "a hearing person without hearing".

Jane said: "I had lost my identity; everyone spoke to me through my husband. Even my family kept communication to a minimum; my confidence and self-esteem were at an all-time low. I had always been a 'people person'; now I was lonely, frustrated and depressed and my days were filled with negative thoughts and isolation".

The changes caused by her hearing loss had also affected Jane's family, who didn't know how to cope.

In 1998, East Durham Deafened & Hearing Impaired Support (EDDHIS) was formed and charitable status was gained. The first Local Community Support Group was set up in Horden with four other people living in Easington who didn't fit into the hard of hearing clubs or deaf clubs. The support group became a vital part of the life of everyone who wished to reintegrate back into society and has since become the model for a network of advocacy, support and self-help groups across County Durham.

In 2002, funding was acquired from Northern Rock for a full-time development worker and Lloyds TSB funded the running costs of an office in Peterlee. The group rapidly expanded into neighbouring villages.

By 2006, there were seven support groups available across County Durham. All these groups had a lip-reading class with a tutor who was trained through ALTA (Association of Lip-reading Teachers to Adults).

Support for the running of groups within their own districts came from Easington and Sedgefield PCTs. 95% of members were visited in their homes or supported by the Outreach Worker before joining the group and this work is ongoing.

Due to the demand for the services of EDDHIS from across the county it was agreed it should become Durham Deafened Support (DDS) and extend services and membership across the whole of County Durham

Early in 2007, with funding from the Neighbourhood Renewal Service Improvement Fund, an office manager was appointed.

The organisation currently provides lip-reading and other courses of direct benefit to people who have lost their hearing. In addition, it acts as an advocacy service and pressure group for deafened people, pestering all sorts of organisations and people, including me in the past, to ensure they are included in activities most of us would regard as normal. Only one other such organisation exists in the country.

Durham Deafened Support involves volunteers, but it is clear that its existence was due to various funding streams that will now become harder to access.

I do not profess to have looked at all the efforts to provide local involvement and accountability in the Easington area. I have concentrated on the Monitoring and Advisory Board, which covers the whole area, and projects in Blackhall, Horden and Easington Colliery. There are other activities and schemes happening, but what I have looked at gives an idea of the sort of developments which are taking place. Local enthusiasm and initiative enables projects to take place which probably would not happen in a centrally organised monolithic NHS.

Other NHS resources available in the Easington District, apart from Healthworks which has been described, are the Peterlee Community Hospital, which provides outreach clinics in children's and adolescent services, diabetes, gastroenterology and hepatology, geriatrics, orthopaedics, rheumatology, respiratory medicine and urology, as well as providing space for a GP surgery. There is also a highly successful urgent care centre, one of the first in the country. It is not really a base, however, for voluntary or community activity but a valuable resource.

A new Primary Care Centre has just opened in Seaham (2012) This is proposed to provide outreach services in the same way as Peterlee, together with GP surgeries and an urgent care centre, but in addition it draws on the experience of Healthworks to provide bases for community health activities, such as a healthy cooking group. As yet I cannot assess its success.

## Funding issues

But one point must be made every clearly before we run away with an idea that some sort of 'big society' can replace the NHS. All these projects need money. The Health Forums are only effective if they are given support from the NHS. The Hospital of God has its own resources, but is already feeling the effects of reductions in NHS and social services funding on its activities. Healthworks receives substantial funding from the PCT and the local authority, as well as resources from Northumbria Water and what it can access from other sources. The public health budget is to be handed to the local authority, but they will not have the amount the PCT had because some will have to go to the centrally run

Public Health England. The PCT is to be abolished and funding given directly to the Clinical Commissioning Groups. The local authority is in the process of making large cuts. In this climate it is likely Healthworks' budget will be diminished at least.

One of the ideas of the new reforms is for commissioners to be more stringent about value for money. If projects which can mobilise voluntary effort and carry out projects to both promote good health and support those with long-term conditions lose their support, either these activities will have to be funded in some other way, or simply not happen at all. Not only will valuable activities be withdrawn, but direct involvement and a feeling of accountability by the public will no longer be there. I think the consequences of such a move could be far-reaching, and I shall explore them more later in the book.

*Several points emerge from this chapter:*

- *The Easington example indicates that it is far easier for a smaller rather than a larger NHS organisation to be closely involved with its local community.*

- *Community groups can achieve a large amount, particularly if they are properly supported. Their big strength is that they can reach groups which the official apparatus finds difficult, and this is particularly desirable when encouraging healthy lifestyles.*

- *Semi-independent groups can often work with excluded groups, and also represent them. This produces the situation where a publicly funded organisation could challenge the NHS about resources and access for those excluded groups.*

- *If public funds are involved there must be proper supervision and accountability.*

- *The groups that I looked at do enable people to have some influence on health policy in their areas. They also increase the confidence and capacity of the individuals involved.*

- *These groups are also particularly vulnerable if funding is cut back.*

# CHAPTER 6

# FOUNDATION TRUSTS

*The idea of Foundation Trusts is often neglected in discussions of involvement and accountability, but they do provide a vehicle for achieving both. The evidence so far is that on many occasions they have not produced significant results, either in terms of improving performance or promoting involvement. All the Trusts in the North East are now Foundation Trusts, and this chapter looks in depth about what has been achieved in Northumberland.*

SO FAR I have looked at aspects of community health – programmes to support healthy living and to provide long-term care. I have not looked at the acute sector – basically, hospitals.

## The development of Foundation Trusts

In 2002, hospitals were invited by the then Secretary of State Alan Milburn to apply to become Foundation Trusts (FTs). To achieve this they had to provide evidence of sound management and financial viability. Once a Foundation Trust was established, it was free to manage its own affairs, but its long-term viability depends on its ability to attract patients and funding from commissioning organisations, currently PCTs and after 2013 Clinical Commissioning Groups. Foundation Trusts recruit members who then elect governors who then appoint the Board. Foundation

Trusts are considered mutual structures akin to co-operatives, where local people, patients and staff can become members and governors and hold the Trust to account. For example, Blackpool Fylde and Wyre Hospitals NHS Foundation Trust has 31 governors, made up of appointed, public and staff governors who act as a key link between patients and the public and the board of directors. Some trusts are more committed to co-operative principles and have even written the Rochdale Principles[63] into their constitution and aspire to work closely and in partnership with other mutual as well as local organisations.

## Monitoring FT performance

At the beginning of March 2012 there were 143 NHS FTs. They are authorised and regulated by Monitor, the independent regulator of NHS Foundation Trusts. They include acute trusts, mental health, community and ambulance trusts. A full list of NHS Foundation Trusts can be found on Monitor's website. With the authorisation of North East Ambulance Service in November 2011, the North East became the first region with all trusts having gained Foundation Trust status.

A study undertaken in 2005 by the King's Fund of Homerton University Hospital NHS Foundation Trust found some governors disappointed and disillusioned.[64] A Homerton University Hospital governor said: "I regret to say that I wouldn't be able to pinpoint a particular point or issue that I have been able to achieve by my being a governor." A further study in 2005 by the Nuffield Foundation, written by Patricia Day, a senior research fellow, and Rudolf Klein, emeritus professor, at Bath University's Centre for the Analysis of Social Policy, casts doubt on the government's claim that FTs hand power to local people and represent "a new form of social ownership."[65] "It presents a mixed picture, with many examples of Trusts having poor turnout in elections, and little meaningful engagement by governors." The writers do comment, however, that it was too early to make an effective judgement as the trusts had only been operating for two years.

In July 2011, a further study was published under the auspices of the Nuffield Trust and York University (Verzulli, Jacobs and

Goddard 2011[66]). There was now data from a cohort of 137 FTs available for analysis, rather than the first few hospitals to achieve status, which meant more meaningful results could be produced.. This showed that the better figures recorded by the first trusts to reach foundation status, were due to factors already in place before the introduction of the FT initiative. This is also the likely reason that they were quick to gain trust status. The initial promising results were thus not repeated by all the other trusts which eventually were given permission to become FTs. It remains to be seen if this way of lessening of state interference brings about any benefits which offset these greater costs of salaries and regulation. Commenting on the research, Professor Goddard said:

> "Reducing the role of state involvement in public sector services is part of a broader strategy and may well bring wider benefits to communities, but it is not a costless activity. The governance arrangements for Foundation Trusts have not been trivial and investment has been required to establish new regulatory structures in order to monitor them.
>
> The experience in the health sector suggests that such costs cannot necessarily be set against expectations of enhanced performance."[67]

In other words, establishing Foundation Trust status has little impact on performance, but could have other benefits. Some of the other research indicates that many FTs have not involved their members very effectively. The Health and Social Care Bill 2012 proposes that all NHS trusts become NHS Foundation Trusts or part of an existing NHS Foundation Trust by April 2014.

It is difficult to assess whether the actual introduction of Foundation Trust status has by itself improved performance, since, as the evidence seems to demonstrate, those hospitals which were already well run were more likely to become FTs in the 'first wave'. What is of greater interest to me is whether the change and the talk of cooperative principles actually bring about more involvement and accountability.

What does seem abundantly clear is that the amount of involvement, and whether the Foundation Trust does operate as an organisation responsive to its members, is due to the enthusiasm and commitment of the people in charge. I am aware of some FTs where the commitment is small, and the members are regarded simply as people to attend occasional events so that the Trust can say people are being 'involved'. This bears out some of the research I have quoted above. Members of some Trusts have reported to me anecdotally this is indeed how they feel.

# Integration in Northumberland

As noted above, all the trusts in the North East are now Foundation Trusts. In some areas these trusts are taking over management of the community services, originally organised by primary care trusts. The result is an 'integrated pathway' where community and acute staff work together. There are such arrangements in Teesside, Durham and Northumberland. In Northumberland, social services and NHS community services have been merged into a 'care trust' which is managed by the Foundation Trust – a truly integrated system.

However, there are some rather messy loose ends within the system. The Northumbria Health Trust also includes North Tyneside, where there is a different primary care trust and local authority. Similarly in Durham, the southern and eastern part of the county look to the Hartlepool and Teesside hospital trust, while their community health services are managed by the Durham FT. The integrated pathway works best where there is 'co-terminosity' (a horrible NHS word) between FT catchment areas and local authority boundaries. PCTs usually follow local authority boundaries.

I talked to the Chair of the Northumberland NHS Trust to ascertain how the integrated system worked. Northumberland is regarded as a successful Foundation Trust, and is in the process of taking over the management of the Carlisle and Whitehaven hospitals where there have been problems.

The Northumbria Trust covers three district general hospitals (DGHs) – Ashington (Wansbeck), Hexham and North Tyneside, and seven community hospitals in Alnwick, Berwick, Blyth, Haltwhistle, Morpeth, Rothbury and Sir GB Hunter in Wallsend. In addition it manages hospital, community health and adult social care services in Northumberland and hospital and community health services in North Tyneside. The Trust is in the process of acquiring Carlisle and Whitehaven. In addition, a new specialist emergency care hospital at Cramlington has been given the green light. The hospital is part of the Trust's £200 million investment to improve healthcare for people in Northumberland and North Tyneside. It will be the first in England to have emergency care consultants on site 24 hours a day, seven days a week. There has been considerable support for this initiative from both professionals and the public.[68]

There are still A&E departments at the three DGHs, but they will not deal with 'blue light' once the new emergency care hospital is established. About 80-90% of people make their own way to A&E. Much emergency work is actually done in an ambulance on the way to hospital.

The 'seamless pathways' are in the process of evolving. They will work best where everything is 'co-terminous', as in Northumberland. In other areas there are problems similar to those in County Durham where the management of community services is done by by the North Tees and Hartlepool Foundation Trust on Teesside, but this does not apply to parts of their catchment area in South Durham.

I asked the Chair whether integrating the FT and Community and Social Care Services encouraged the provision of more services in the community, and whether affected hospital services.

He replied that nurses will not be in hospitals 100% of the time. They may spend 10% of their time in the community. He did not see this as problem threatening the continuation of the DGHs. Contrast this with the situation in Co Durham where there are two DGHs and a third hospital, Bishop Auckland, which is a respite and recuperation centre. It provides a specialist rehabilitation centre with high quality facilities, highly skilled nursing and experienced therapists. It is a centre of excellence in low-risk hip and knee replacement operations and a full range of outpatient and diagnostics is also provided for local patients. Increased community services are seen as a threat to this provision.

Governance arrangements in the Northumbria Trust are as follows. There are 70 governors and seven or eight non-execs (directors).There are two councillors, two ex-councillors, one ex-chief executive, one ex-head teacher and a finance person from ONE North East (the development agency which the government is in the process of closing down). These are the 'lay people' appointed to the board by the governors. The Appointments Commission has no role to play in a Foundation Trust. The governors are the biggest part of the interview panel for non-execs, who have to reply to public adverts. Executive directors are employees of the Trust. There are five women executive directors. The existing membership is 70,000 with an aim to secure 40,000 in Cumbria. (Compare that to 6,000 in Durham and Darlington.) The population served of Co Durham and Darlington, allowing for people who go to Sunderland and Hartlepool, is roughly comparable to that of the Northumbria Trust (450,000), perhaps slightly more. The Northumbria Trust takes recruiting governors seriously. Most governors have a 'vested interest' in the hospital – they have either received treatment themselves, or members of their family have, they sit on major committees, and there are regular 'breakfast meetings' in different parts of the county for the Chair to meet the governors. There are also governor development meetings. For example, the members, have to vote on the Cumbria merger. The chair sees this membership as a major political force to exert pressure on MPs. The board is considerably influenced by the governors: they are consulted about patient safety issues; they do PEAT (Patient Environment Action Teams) visits, and are vociferous about patients' complaints. Governors sit on committees working with the architect on the emergency care centre. My own personal observation is that the Chair works very hard. He makes it his business to meet all governors and keep them informed of what is happening.

So far as consulting the wider population is concerned, 800 people were involved in meetings about the new facility at Cramlington.

The Trust is making a big effort to engage with the local authority. Representatives will start attending area forums. Non-execs
will also attend local councils and report. There are a large
number of parish councils in Northumberland as well as town
councils. The Chair envisaged the non-exec directors taking a
bigger role in the public engagement planned for North Cumbria,
which is planned to start in the next few months. The Trust will
try to get into council area meetings as a regular performer. I had
an extensive discussion about the involvement of the Trust with
local government. The Chair had been a council leader, and felt
that local government no longer had the power and authority it
once did. He had a vision of the Foundation Trust membership
being a major political force. It could rebuild local government as
something most people engage with. Given the wide responsibilities of the Trust, which is the major employer in Northumberland,
this is a very interesting idea, which I shall develop below.

The Chair did not think that, in a rural trust in a more deprived
part of the country, there was any risk of large-scale privatisation.
(Unless, of course, GPs, who are private contractors, are counted).

A major issue in many rural areas is either the closure or downgrading of district hospitals. This does not seem to be an issue
in Northumberland. Consultants do some work in community
hospitals. I noted that at Haltwhistle there is to be an integrated
development with social services to provide 15 rehabilitation beds
and 12 extra-care flats. This means people requiring long-term
care do not have to stay in an acute hospital but can recuperate
near their own community. A new community hospital is also
planned for Berwick upon Tweed.

## Private provision and patient choice

The Chair did not see private provision as a threat, but more as an
encouragement to the NHS to 'up its game'. This is what happened
during the Blairite era (1997 to 2007), and the general opinion is
that some private provision did encourage the NHS to improve.
We discussed what could happen if the government changed
the rules to break up the present integrated provision and allow
private providers to take the 'good bits'. The Chair felt strongly that

patients must be allowed, however, to choose the care that is best for them. At the moment Northumbria's private 'cap' is set at less than 5%, and the Chair does not know whether North Cumbria has a cap at all. There is much elective care being carried out in the DGHs within the 18-week targets that there does not appear to be any need or incentive to pay. He thinks it will stay that way, but GP reorganisation may encourage more private work. We shall have to see how the consultants reorganise their work. But there has to be 'patient choice'

We had a long discussion about health inequalities. The roots of many of them are in the community. There was a successful project on the Meadowell Estate (an estate on North Tyneside where there were riots in 1991, and there has been considerable regeneration since) where NHS and social care workers worked together. There are also problems of integrated working – management hierarchies, accountability etc. I alluded to these earlier, but the direction of travel now certainly seems to be to try to eliminate these barriers. The Chair thought the 'big society' concept rather naive. It might work in affluent areas, but in deprived ones there are problems of criminality and intimidation. We could have pursued this argument further. Certainly community projects have run in poor areas of County Durham, but they need support.

## Conclusions

The integration of services on a large scale has freed up resources to enable the trust to improve services. This whole idea of integrating health and local government opens up all sorts of possibilities. Good governance and accountability are not just about whether particular boards are elected or appointed. They are about whether ordinary people feel involved or not, and whether there are effective channels for them to influence the large organisations which play a major part in their lives. The Northumbria model requires energy and commitment from the people involved in the trust, but it does seem to be working. The Health and Wellbeing Boards should firmly link the councillors to the NHS providers, so they can pressurise the commissioners, particularly the National Commissioning Board, to meet their needs. MPs should be encouraged to support their constituents in tussles between commissioners and patients/providers. Health will become very political. H&WB Boards should be open to the public and minutes should be discussed by the other councillors. Health will become as important for local government as education and housing.

One issue which will be problematic will be scrutiny. If health and local government become more integrated, it will be difficult for a council to scrutinise itself. The chair suggested individual local authorities scrutinise other ones. That is an interesting idea.

---

*The evidence on the performance of Foundation Trusts so far does not appear to be encouraging. Those involved do not feel very effective or valued, and this is confirmed by evidence from individuals I know personally. To make a Foundation Trust work there must be a strong commitment from the chair, the board and the management. This seems to be the case in Northumberland, whereas it is not elsewhere. The Chair of the Northumberland Trust is a former council leader who has a strong personal commitment to public accountability, whereas many other chairs appear to be people with a more 'manageria' background and outlook. In many cases the FT's principles are not really understood. The membership of Northumberland is over 10 times higher than other FTs in the region, and the trust also performs well, providing services to a mix of rural and urban areas. This makes it a powerful player in the area. Perhaps other FTs could model themselves on examples such as this. An interesting aspect of the Northumberland situation is the close cooperation of community health, acute provision and social care. The trust also works closely with the local authority. This seems to be a way forward for securing both community involvement and accountability.*

# CHAPTER 7

# TACKLING HEALTH INEQUALITIES

*A socialist approach to health must confront the issue of health inequalities. The previous government showed much more enthusiasm for tackling the issue than the present one. Although overall standards of health have improved since the introduction of the NHS, many studies have shown that relative inequalities have not.*

*Health inequalities are caused by many factors outside the NHS's overall control, but intervention at a micro level can alleviate them. Involving the wider public is often the only way to do this, and the chapter looks at possible approaches.*

WE HAVE stated in Chapter 2 that the reduction of health inequalities has been and should continue to be a core principle of Labour's vision for the NHS. It is easy to state the aim. How to realise it in practice is the problem.

There is a danger with studies such as 'The Spirit Level' by Wilkinson and Pickett [69] is that their solutions are what I would call 'structural' – a more equal society would produce more equal health outcomes. That is probably so, but it is also rather utopian. Producing a more equal society may take a long time, and health problems affect people here and now. In any case, if we cannot solve them the NHS will not be able to cope in the future. We have to consider whether we can reduce health inequalities in the social situation we have now.

As Professor Bambra has recently pointed out, the way funding is distributed can either reduce or enlarge health inequalities. [70] She has calculated that an 'age only' distribution of resources, as distinct from an allocation which currently links to deprivation indices, could lead to a 14.9% loss of resources in the North East (or £265 per head), with the South Central area gaining 15.8% (or £220 per head). Such a change would undoubtedly make health inequalities worse, and Professor Bambra points out that it would also have political ramifications (benefitting Conservative areas at the cost of Labour ones). But the unfortunate fact remains that with the present distribution of resources there are substantial inequalities, and what can be done at the micro level to address them?

In his recent paper for the Policy Network, 'A Left Trilemma' (2012)[71] Peter Taylor-Gooby discusses the concept of 'pre-distribution' as distinct from 'redistribution'.

"The grand tradition of state welfare has rested on redistribution through taxation of the better off or of individuals at life-cycle stages when income exceeds resources, to provide welfare when they are in need. Pre-distribution addresses inequalities at source, through state interventions into the operation of market systems to reduce income inequalities and shift power towards the lower paid.

The most powerful arguments for this approach rest on the claim that state welfare was most successful in the UK when the institutions to reinforce pre-distribution were at their strongest, in the 1950s and 1960s. The American scholar Jacob Hacker points out that the massive increase in inequality in some of the most developed countries is associated with erosion of the protective institutional framework."

# Health inequality policies and strategies

Policies such as taxing the rich and supporting the poor try to equalise outcomes. Policies of 'pre-distribution' try to even the playing field so that the poorer in society are in a stronger bargaining position to begin with.

Commentators from the Black Report[72] onwards have pointed out that the better-educated and better-off traditionally use the health system for their own benefit. They are in a better position to debate with professionals and to ensure they receive the best treatment. The 'community development' approach to improving public health (and thereby reducing health inequalities) aims to encourage volunteers and community groups to organise their own projects and to encourage others to change their lifestyles. These projects not only improve the health of those involved, but they also increase their self-confidence and organising ability. They are then better able to both use the resources available more effectively and demand more for their areas.

It was noted in Chapter 6 that the Northumberland Care Trust had recruited 70,000 members. The Chair commented that if these people could be organised they could become a powerful political force to demand better health resources. If the parliamentary victory in Wyre Forest on a hospital closure issue by Dr. Richard Taylor in 2001[73] is anything to go by, this is something which politicians cannot ignore. Thus involving people effectively in health organisations can reduce health inequalities.

How the NHS organises itself can encourage effective public involvement too. In the north east there has been a successful anti-smoking campaign called 'Fresh'.[74] This was a campaign established in the North East in 2005 as Smoke Free North East, and then became Fresh Smoke Free North East (SFNE) in 2006. The 'SFNE model' is described by Russell *et al* (2009)[75] as one where different agencies work together, primary care trusts, local authorities and community organisations. They make two important points:

(1)  It maintains an identity that is separate from the NHS, despite its funding. This is underscored by its location in government

offices in the centre of the region and by its governance arrangements.

(2) Its quasi-independence gives it scope to act as a lobbying organisation.

The salient point of this strategy was that an independent agency was set up as a result of collaboration between different NHS departments and local government. This was then able to operate with a significant degree of independence.

Fresh is still operating, although its funding may be at risk. The agency is judged to have been a success, in that smoking has reduced. The North East saw the biggest regional drop in smoking nationwide between 2005-2009, when smoking dropped from 29% to 22%. (These figures are from the General Lifestyle Survey, ONS, 2010.) Fresh's website states:

> "In the North East more women that men smoke – 23% of women compared to 20% of men. However, this compares with 42% of men and 36% of women in 1980 which highlights how smoking rates have declined. The overall decrease in smoking prevalence seems to be mainly due to the increase in people who have never smoked or only occasionally smoked. The proportion of adults who have never smoked or only occasionally smoked has been rising steadily, from 43% in 1982 to 53% in 2008. In 2008, those aged 20-24 and 25-34 reported the highest prevalence of cigarette smoking (32% and 27% respectively), while those aged 60 and over reported the lowest prevalence."

Commenting on the success of the agency, Russell *et al* state:

> "However, our research demonstrates that the SFNEO is unique in terms of its multiple sources of statutory funding and its ability to act as a quasi-independent, campaigning organization able to bring unusual partners together to lobby where other organisations and individuals might otherwise have been prevented or discouraged from doing so.

Its focus on social norm change, manifested through its extensive use of media agencies and social marketing, has been another unique and pioneering feature of SFNEO in its early years."

In a way, the Fresh strategy is another version of community engagement, although on a large scale. An agency engaged with the North East, and brought other people in, so as to gain the maximum effect. It also employed techniques such as social marketing to reach groups who might not otherwise have been engaged.

It is hoped to apply the same approach to Balance, another unique agency in the North East which is aiming to reduce alcohol consumption. [76]

Balance is funded by the North East's PCTs and also receives support from the North East Police Forces with a full-time seconded police officer leading on the crime and disorder programme.

The organisation also brings together a number of other partners and stakeholders including:

- Local authorities;

- Health services;

- Police forces;

- Emergency services;

- Voluntary agencies;

- Alcohol support groups;

- Treatment services;

- Prison and probation services.

*(Source: Balance North East website)*

In some ways the task of Balance is harder, because its message is less clear. Fresh was attempting to stop smoking altogether, whereas Balance is attempting to reduce and moderate alcohol consumption. Fresh contributed to the implementation of the smoking ban, and Balance is one of the agencies lobbying for a minimum alcohol price.

Thus, joint working by the NHS with other agencies and a determined effort to involve communities can pay off, as the approach of Fresh has shown. The North East here has established a model for others to follow. Such agencies, must, however, be given freedom of manoeuvre and the power to use propaganda and lobby, as Fresh and Balance are successfully doing. Perhaps the same approach can be adopted for obesity.

# Local level action

Action can be taken at the grassroots level too. Public Health is to be transferred from the PCT to Durham County Council. The Council has published its strategy for dealing with health inequalities.

> "It will be an asset-based approach and co-production and will require ownership by partner organisations and the health networks. In addition, partners must be willing to share power and control and help the community to do things itself. Clearly, this will require a shift in current approaches to improving health outcomes and will require considerable discussion to facilitate full understanding of the approach. Some partners will recognise the approach and its links to community development: it is clearly not new but its use to tackle health inequalities is a relatively recent development in England."

> *(Durham County Council, Health and Wellbeing Partnership, 2011)*

The asset-based approach is set out in an IDEA pamphlet published in 2010, 'A glass half-full: how an asset approach can improve community health and well-being'. [77]

The pamphlet argues that the only effective way to mobilise communities to confront health inequalities, is to look at what they have, rather than what they lack:

> "A growing body of evidence shows that when practitioners begin with a focus on what communities have (their assets)

as opposed to what they don't have (their needs) a community's efficacy in addressing its own needs increases, as does
its capacity to lever in external support. It provides healthy
community practitioners with a fresh perspective on building bridges with socially excluded people and marginalised
groups."

This approach has also been described as 'co-production', where
professionals work together with the people in the community
rather than simply telling them what to do, seeing them as partners rather than clients. [78]

It appears then that it is possible for health agencies to take
action to reduce health inequalities at a local level. There are three
objectives for such a policy.

(1) One is to empower those who are disadvantaged in society to
use the health system more to their advantage;

(2) The second is to encourage people to change their behaviour
when it contributes to bad health;

(3) The third is to provide long-term care for those with long-
term conditions which have to be managed rather than cured.

All require engagement with communities. Building up disadvantaged communities will empower them and make them more
able to deal with their problems. Community groups must take
ownership of strategies to encourage healthy lifestyles. People will
not change their behaviour if they feel they are being bullied or
lectured. Finally, volunteer groups must be properly resourced
and supported if they are to provide support and encouragement
for those with long-term conditions, and also enable those people
to be properly included in society. Durham Deafened support
group is a good example of this. It not only helps and supports
deafened people, but campaigns for them to be properly included
in society.

Such strategies can be at a community level, or they can be
regional as Fresh has been. The essential point about larger-scale
initiatives is that they work cooperatively with other agencies and
take people and communities with them.

Thus although it may not be possible to totally 'solve' the problem of health inequalities, determined efforts by the NHS working with other agencies, and, most importantly, engaging the community, can reduce them.

*There are structural and funding issues which a future Labour government will hopefully address which will reduce health inequalities. Of particular importance is how funding is distributed between the various parts of the country. Nevertheless, the experience of the past 60 years has been that funding alone will not of itself solve the problem. Dealing with health inequalities means empowering the most vulnerable in society – the concept of 'pre-distribution'. These groups are often excluded from much NHS activity and unlikely to engage in programmes to improve public health. One way is to engage with community organisations which are more likely to influence excluded groups. Joint initiatives such as Fresh which, although funded largely by the NHS, acts independently of it, seem to have had an effect on reducing smoking.*

*Such an approach means effectively engaging with people and regarding them as resources, not problems.*

# CHAPTER 8

# THE ROLE OF LOCAL AUTHORITIES IN HEALTH

> *Local authorities have always had a role in health, and the recent proposals to restore public health to them will increase this. The terms of reference of the Health and Wellbeing Boards give substantial powers over commissioning and local health provision. Foundation Trusts can also involve large numbers of people if they take membership recruiting seriously. This chapter considers whether these developments can substantially improve local involvement in health service provision.*

LOCAL AUTHORITIES have always been involved with health. Pre-1948 they managed a range of hospitals, although as Timmins says in 'The Five Giants – A Biography of the Welfare State' (1995): "They tended to be the less good ones – ex workhouses, mental health illness 'bins' and the fever and TB isolation hospitals." Much of public health was run by local authorities, who appointed a Medical Officer of Health. This position continued until the reforms of 1974, which transferred public health responsibilities to the NHS. A Director of Public Health position was created. This position became a joint appointment with local authorities in 2006 when PCTs were made co-terminous with them. Under the 2012

Act, directors of Public Health will once again be appointments by local authorities.

It is important to get things in perspective. The amount allocated to public health as part of the total NHS budget is small – something like 4%, and the total budget for social care is £17 billion for 2010-11 (DoH), compared to a total NHS budget for last year of £114 billion. Thus the amounts that local authorities will spend on health if social care is included will be significantly less than the NHS budget.

Estimates vary, but between 60 and 80% of the total NHS budget will be handed over to the clinical commissioning groups (CCGs).This is where the real power will lie. Thus, for local authorities to have influence there must be proper liaison between the commissioning groups and the local authority.

## Health and Wellbeing Boards

There is a framework for this. The 2012 Act requires all local authorities (upper tier where the two-tier system still exists) to establish Health and Wellbeing Boards (HWBs). [79] The powers of these have been strengthened following the listening exercise and subsequent debate about the bill, but as yet they are untested in practice.

The HWBs will consist of at least one councillor, but local authorities can have a majority on the board if they wish, the director of children's services, the director of public health, a representative of Healthwatch (the successor to LINks), a representative from each CCG, a representative of the NHS Commissioning Board, and "other such persons as the local authority thinks appropriate".

The HWBs have to produce a 'Joint Strategic Needs Assessment' which will result in a strategy. CCGs will be 'strongly expected' to follow this. As the BMA guidance points out, their powers on paper will be quite extensive:

> "The role of Health and Wellbeing Board will extend beyond guiding and monitoring the commissioning process. The Government envisages Health and Wellbeing Boards playing a bigger role in promoting joint commissioning. Health and Wellbeing Boards will be able to lead joint commissioning

for specific services, if the local authority and CCGs wish to delegate responsibility.

An example of such an area could be the joint commissioning of health and social care for people with dementia.

The Government has made provision in the legislation for Health and Wellbeing Boards to input into wider policy areas such as housing, the environment and education, with the aim of promoting a cohesive health improvement strategy across the local authority agenda. The Bill also makes provision for a local authority to arrange for a Health and Wellbeing Board to 'exercise any other functions of the authority'.

*(Health and Wellbeing Boards, GPC guidance, BMA, September 2011)*

There is considerable scepticism by some about the actual role of the HWBs, that they will simply be a talking-shop without any real clout. It is up to the local authorities to take them seriously, and ensure that some committed members sit on them. Liz Kendall, a member of the shadow health team has recently expressed this view.

## Breaking down silos

What are important are the provisions to extend the remit of health into other departments such as housing, the environment and education. This is an attempt to break down the 'silo mentality' which often prevails in local government. The last government launched the 'Total Place' initiative in March 2010 in an attempt to the very same thing.[80]

"Total Place is a new initiative that looks at how a 'whole area' approach to public services can lead to better services at less cost. It seeks to identify and avoid overlap and duplication between organisations – delivering a step change in both service improvement and efficiency at the local level, as well as across Whitehall."

*(Leadership Centre for Local Government)*

It was piloted in 13 local government areas, but the present government has discontinued it. The vision of the strategy was very ambitious.

> "The evidence base from the pilots outlined in this report provides a strong platform for us to take radical, but also practical, steps for the future. It sets out the case for change, at local level and on a national scale, which can deliver true transformation in public services across the country. It shows that real savings can be made through the Total Place approach. It also makes clear the need for strong local leadership, with local authorities playing a pivotal role in delivering radical improvements in services, with their partners, through the single offer, innovative policy offer and a range of other initiatives that build on the pilots' findings." (HM Treasury and Department of Communities and Local Government, March 2010)

Essentially, it was about trying to join up services and merge 'back office' functions. It is interesting that one of the departments sponsoring the White Paper was HM Treasury, not renowned for new initiatives which will cost money. The words 'value for money' appear frequently, and there is nothing wrong with that. We all pay tax, or at least most of us ordinary people do. It seems that the proposals for the Health and Wellbeing Boards are returning to the same idea; that health and other services should work together.

I talked to the current cabinet member for health at Durham County Council. She is a real whirlwind of energy, and discussed the various community development initiatives she has begun in her ward with the objective of promoting better health. Her ward is isolated, with no big supermarket or leisure centre within easy distance, so she has helped establish various initiatives to bulk-buy food, build playgrounds, and organise a healthy eating group. All these involve partnership working with other groups to draw down additional funding.

She was also very keen on the idea, as expressed in the guidance to the Health and Wellbeing Boards, to work with other council departments to promote health issues. She thought every council employee should have a duty to promote good health.

# Integrating community health and social care services

There is considerable support amongst health professionals for the closer integration of community health services with social care. At the moment, community health services are still the responsibility of the PCTs, but the actual running of them has in many cases been commissioned to Foundation Trusts (as is the case in Durham, Northumberland and North Tees). Social care is run by the county council. It is a particular issue for support for people with long-term conditions, such as chronic mental health problems, diabetes and chronic obstructive pulmonary disease. If these conditions could be more effectively treated and supported in the community people would not have to visit, or remain in, hospital so much, or in extreme cases be re-referred. For a fuller debate of the issue, see 'Where Next for the NHS Reforms?' by Chris Ham et al, The Kings Fund, 2011. [81] Their view is that:

> "This model of integrated care would focus much more on preventing ill health, supporting self-care, enhancing primary care, providing care in people's homes and the community, and increasing co-ordination between primary care teams and specialists and between health and social care."

There are many barriers to the total integration of the two services. In some areas, such as Northumberland, a joint community health and social care trust has been set up. As the Director of Public Health at Durham pointed out to me, there is a difference of philosophy. Health is a universal service, whereas social services are means-tested. There is also a concern amongst health professionals that resources could be diverted from health to social care in a bid to balance budgets. Nevertheless, if actual integration of services is not possible, as the Kings Fund points out, there can be "virtual or contractual" integration in which providers work together through networks and alliances. An organisational merger does not necessarily deliver benefits without clinical and service integration, which can be achieved by joint working on the ground.

Local authorities frequently restructure by transferring teams to different departments, but it does not necessarily mean they work better together unless there is a mechanism to make them do so. Joint commissioning and the powers of the HWB could do this.

So far this discussion has looked at the role of the HWB and the integration of social care and health. I have discussed the role public health could play in reducing health inequalities if it worked alongside other local government and community bodies to follow a community development strategy in the previous chapter. Both the Director of Public Health and the cabinet member for health in Durham seem fully signed up for this strategy. But the question needs to be posed as to whether local authorities see themselves as playing a major role in health.

## The role of local authorities

Local authorities currently operate Health and Social Care Scrutiny Committees. (OSCs) These have a particular duty to ensure that the NHS carries out proper consultations when there is a major restructuring of a service. In the original draft of the bill it was proposed that they be abolished because they would be replaced by the HWBs. The HWBs will be organising the commissioning of services, so it is not easy for them to scrutinise themselves. The Local Government Association made representations to keep Health OSCs, and they succeeded. Some local authorities take their duties more seriously than others. Durham has developed a robust Health and Social Care OSC, which has had recent successes in making sure the NHS did a proper consultation about the relocation of mental health services, and also conducted a full scale investigation of the conversion of Bishop Auckland hospital into a respite and recuperation centre which was acknowledged as an example of good practice. [82] The only problem with the OSCs is they are much better at scrutinising outside agencies than their own council. The OSC at Durham spends far more time on dealing with the NHS than social care.

There have been suggestions that one council should scrutinise another to ensure the process is more independent, but I shall not pursue this debate at present. The issue for local authorities is whether they wish to simply scrutinise health services, or actually take a role in organising them.

When I talked to the Chair of the Northumberland NHS trust, he saw greater involvement in health as a way of reviving local government. It is true that the powers of local government have been reduced in many areas, notably education, by successive governments, and there has been a reluctance to hand them more powers in matters such as transport regulation and provision. In the case of health local authorities are acquiring more powers and responsibilities. If the proposed duties of the HWBs are actually translated into practice their powers will be considerable over health.

As I mentioned earlier, the Northumberland Trust has been particularly successful, not only in recruiting members, but also effectively involving them. There is no other organisation in the area which engages so many people. The Chair felt that if the trust and the local authority effectively worked together, there would be a large accountable organisation delivering public services in touch with a large number of people. The questions are, how do you do it and do you want to do it?

## Conclusions

After considering various examples of good practice across the North East of England I am optimistic about what we can do and to what a future Labour government should commit itself. I have met many people committed to the ideals of public service who do not want services privatised in this area, and here we have a model of what a publicly-run health system could look like. We have to recognise that in the future the demands on the NHS will grow and the resources available to it are likely to be constrained. The pressure will be to integrate 'back office', to work collaboratively, and not only improve the service but save money. Integration of management and services could both improve health outcomes and save money. We also want to get rid of any top-down bureaucracy which is out of touch with ordinary people and effectively engage them. It is the people's NHS and they are being asked to pay for it through taxes. Although there is a scope for the use of the private sector to provide services if the NHS fails or does not have the resources or expertise, wholesale privatisation will undermine the integrated, publicly accountable model to which we aspire.

In my final two chapters I want to draw together some conclusions from my investigations and map out a way forward.

*This chapter has shown that considerable opportunities exist through the new Health and Wellbeing Boards for the commissioning process and local government to work together. The powers of the HWBs could enable them to integrate local services and produce value for money as well as better outcomes, as the previous government's 'Total Place' initiative aspired to do. NHS Foundation Trusts can involve large numbers of people if they try hard enough, and by working together with local authorities and the GP commissioners they could not only enable there to be a real public input into health, but also benefit the health service by enabling them to reach far more people to explain what their objectives are. The big question is, will local government in particular seize the opportunities which are being offered?*

# CHAPTER 9

## INTERNATIONAL COMPARISONS

> *The discussion in this book so far has centred on England. There are differences in the way the NHS is run in Scotland and Wales, but the same issues which have been raised will be relevant there. International comparisons can be helpful, but will only be useful if done with other developed countries. This chapter can only look superficially at what is a complicated subject, but hopefully can produce some useful conclusions.*

THE BEST source to use for statistical data is the OECD.[83] The latest figures available for 2010 are given below.

| Country | % of GDP spent on health | Life expectancy (years) |
|---|---|---|
| Australia | 9.1 | 81.8 |
| Austria | 11.0 | 80.7 |
| Belgium | 10.5 | 80.3 |
| Canada | 11.4 | 80.8 |
| Chile | 8.0 | 79.0 |
| Czech Republic | 7.5 | 77.7 |
| Denmark | 11.1 | 79.3 |
| Estonia | 6.3 | 75.6 |
| Finland | 8.9 | 80.2 |
| France | 11.6 | 81.3 |
| Germany | 11.6 | 80.5 |
| Greece | 10.2 | 80.6 |
| Hungary | 7.8 | 74.3 |
| Iceland | 9.3 | 81.5 |
| Ireland | 9.2 | 81.0 |
| Israel | 7.9 | 81.7 |
| Italy | 9.3 | 82.0 |
| Japan | 9.5 | 83.0 |
| Korea | 7.1 | 80.7 |
| Luxembourg | 7.9 | 80.7 |
| Mexico | 6.2 | 75.5 |
| Netherlands | 12.0 | 80.8 |
| New Zealand | 10.1 | 81.0 |
| Norway | 9.4 | 81.2 |
| Poland | 7.0 | 76.3 |
| Portugal | 10.7 | 79.8 |
| Slovak Republic | 9.0 | 75.2 |
| Slovenia | 9.0 | 79.5 |
| Spain | 9.6 | 82.2 |
| Sweden | 9.6 | 81.5 |
| Switzerland | 11.4 | 82.6 |
| Turkey | 6.1 | 74.3 |
| United Kingdom | 9.6 | 80.6 |
| United States | 17.6 | 78.7 |
| OECD average | 9.5 | 79.8 |

Looking at these figures, several points emerge:

- Life expectancy in the UK is slightly above the OECD average, and expenditure almost the same as the average.

- The United States spends significantly more on healthcare than all the other OECD countries, but does not seem to achieve better outcomes. Spain achieves longer life expectancy for roughly the same outlay as the UK.

- Japan has the longest life expectancy, and only an average outlay on health.

- The Scandinavian countries seem to achieve better outcomes for relatively modest expenditure.

- Switzerland spends proportionately more than these countries, but only achieves slightly better outcomes.

- Despite its difficulties, Greece does well.

There are many factors which affect health. Wilkinson and Pickett (2009) argue that Scandinavian countries and Japan have better health outcomes because they are more equal societies. [84] There may be other factors such as climate or diet. What I am interested in is whether we can learn from overseas systems which produce better results in a fair way.

Norway and Spain both achieve better outcomes than the UK for less resource, so it is worth 'drilling down' to see whether there are reasons for this. Spain attributes its good health to both diet and climate, but it also has a free healthcare system similar to ours. There are also more trained doctors per head of population. Norway, on the other hand, has both more doctors and considerably more nurses per head of population (14.4 per 100, compared to 9.6 in the UK). The Norwegians put far more emphasis on healthy lifestyles, and have low rates of obesity and diabetes. They also have a publicly funded health system like ours, with more resources, often provided by nurses, in the community.

Britain has world-class hospitals of which we are justly very proud. But we appear to have neglected community health services. The countries which can deliver best results seem to have more resources 'on the ground', encouraging healthy lifestyles. I should emphasise that more work needs to be done considering international comparisons.

An interesting fact is that countries with good health outcomes, Spain, Norway and Japan, all have publicly run and accessible health systems. Japan has compulsory insurance, but fees are regulated by the government and hospitals must be non-profit making institutions run by physicians.

This contrasts with America and Switzerland where costs are much higher compared to outcomes.

A feature of the British system is that you can only be admitted to hospital if referred by a GP. In America anyone can admit themselves, provided they wish to pay. The majority of Americans have some form of health insurance, either provided personally or through their employers. One of the reasons for the high costs is the legal fees of the insurance companies suing providers. The present Democratic administration is attempting to require all Americans to have health insurance, and assisting with the costs for those who cannot afford it. Another feature of the American system is Medicare, which pays fees for those over 65 (although there are limitations). Overall, it is an open-ended system, without tight controls on costs. A concern of many is that with the new commissioning system a legal culture may enter our system. The *Newcastle Journal* reported on July 11$^{th}$ 2012 that Newcastle Hospitals Foundation Trust may make a legal challenge to a commissioning decision by NHS North of Tyne to take a service away from one of their hospitals. [85]

The Swiss system has similarities. All citizens are obliged to have private health insurance. Again, costs seem to escalate.

---

*Two conclusions can be drawn from this admittedly brief survey of other health systems.*

*(1) Publicly run systems where costs are controlled seem to do better compared to 'open ended' private insurance schemes.*

*(2) Health is better where more resources are put into community services aimed at providing better health. Having good hospitals does not necessarily mean good health outcomes overall.*

---

# CHAPTER 10

# THE CONCLUSION: PULLING
# EVERYTHING TOGETHER

*This chapter considers the direction of travel for a future government which is committed to the NHS. It is likely such a government will be Labour, or one where the Labour Party has the leading role. A commitment to a publicly-run service which serves the public does not mean one which is centrally directed with little local accountability of scope for local initiatives. Health services should encourage public involvement, and there are examples of where this has been done. This is both to encourage schemes to improve public health, and to explain why changes need to be made. Local government and the NHS should work more closely together. Such approaches could reduce inequalities at a local level.*

*There may be problems regarding private provisions and local authorities that do not wish or are not able to provide good public services, and these issues are addressed.*

I REALISE that this book which began with my observations about a County Durham village has since covered a great deal of ground. What can we draw out from this to give us an idea about the direction of travel for a future government which, unlike this one appears to be, is committed to the future of the National Health Service?

A concern that I have is that people who desperately want to defend the NHS have an image of it which is often out of date. It is easy to campaign against a hospital closure, particularly if you live in an isolated and deprived community, and it sometimes appears almost treacherous to question whether we need as many hospitals as we have now. This is a particular problem in the North East, where informed opinion generally agrees that there are too many hospitals for the population.

# NHS challenges and solutions

The challenges facing the NHS today are illnesses which are the result of social conditions and lifestyles, and also the cost of providing care and support for an ageing population. Health inequalities stubbornly persist. This does not mean there will be no need for hospitals, but fewer and more sophisticated acute ones. Smaller community hubs with beds will be able to cope with patients who cannot be discharged, but currently fill up acute beds because there are not facilities for them in the community. There should be more such facilities. The present policy of discharging people as quickly as possible often causes considerable distress, and if the right support is not there, means people are soon back again. Paradoxically, concentration on fewer high-tech acute centres could result in more beds being available locally than there are now. The Northumberland example gives an idea of the way forward. Much more care will have to be delivered locally, which will require better resources and trained staff than we have now.

What is also abundantly clear from the work I have done is that these challenges will involve all of us. They are not something which can simply be left to a few professionals, but it is possible to make progress when community resources are mobilised, as in the case of Fresh, the campaign to reduce smoking in the North East. Mobilising community resources does not mean spending less money. It could mean spending more, but it means giving more of it, and more control, to local communities. Resources must be distributed more fairly between areas, as Professor Bambra and many others have pointed out, but they also need to be distributed down to the front line if there is to be progress in dealing with health inequalities.

A recent news report (BBC, April 25th 2012) refers to a report in the Journal of Diabetic Medicine. [86] The report calls for far more action at a community level. I give a brief extract below.

> "The majority of NHS spending on diabetes is avoidable, says a report in the journal Diabetic Medicine. It suggests that 80% of the NHS's £9.8bn annual UK diabetes bill goes on the cost of treating complications. Experts say much of this is preventable with health checks and better education – something the Department of Health says it is tackling.
>
> The report also predicts that by 2035, diabetes will cost the NHS £16.8bn, 17% of its entire budget. Baroness Barbara Young, from Diabetes UK – one of the charities involved in the Impact Diabetes report – said: 'The report shows that without urgent action, the already huge sums of money spent on treating diabetes will rise to unsustainable levels that threaten to bankrupt the NHS.'"

The report was authored by the York Health Economic Consortium and developed in partnership between Diabetes UK, JDRF and Sanofi.

This shows the challenge the NHS is facing. Better health education will come up against the problem which I have highlighted in the study. Some people will take no notice, particularly when they are pressurised by a powerful food industry and tasty food is a comfort for an otherwise depressing life. Communities have to fight back, like the one in County Durham has done, but they need support to do it. There also need to be powerful agencies like Fresh which can mobilise community resources.

## Devolving power

I have stressed in my research the increased role for local government in health, and how this could be expanded further. This is a challenge local government should take up. They frequently bemoan loss of power and influence, and the growing dominance of Whitehall, but here is an opportunity where they could gain more power and influence over something of considerable importance to the communities they serve. Hopefully, it would reverse the decline in interest in local elections. People are more likely to vote for something they see as important and leading to results they can see in their own area. As the Director of Public Health for Durham said to me, local authorities are better at involving local communities than the NHS is.

This is not really the fault of the NHS. When it began it had clear tasks to perform. It had to re-equip hospitals and deal with contagious diseases. This required a centralised control system – Bevan's famous quip about the "sound of a bedpan dropped in Tredegar will echo through Whitehall". Although management of the NHS has been decentralised, it still has a culture of command and control. A senior NHS executive once said to me that "health was too important to be entrusted to local government".

Really devolving power, and sharing it with local authorities will require a massive cultural change, and in some ways a leap of faith, but it is something which must be done. This does not mean a dilution of expertise, or lack of tight control on spending. But it does mean letting communities in if we are to tackle the problems we face. An NHS which took involvement seriously working together with local government could be a very effective mechanism for really involving people in something which is of the utmost importance – health – and also interest them in the other functions of local government too.

## Changing cultures

Not only the NHS but also local government has to change its culture. The whole idea behind the new Health and Wellbeing Boards is that the two should work together. I have sat on the Health Scrutiny Committee, on and off, since it was set up in 2002, and have seen it develop. The officers have gained considerable expertise, and much useful work has been done jointly between the local authority and the NHS. Both sides have learnt to trust each other more. But some councillors still see it in a confrontational way. They see their role to criticise the NHS and attack it on issues relating to service changes.

The NHS for its part has not been good at consultation. Although busy staff are aware of the need to involve the public, many of them do not really know how to do so and see it as an unwelcome distraction. They are often keen to offload the process and use any available avenue to be able to say it has been done. This results in the public seeing a badly handled consultation as an attempt to deceive them. They often feel that the decision has already been made. There is a fundamental matter of principle here. People should not be given the impression that they are making a decision if they are not. For example, there may be good clinical reasons for closing a particular unit because it is no longer fit for purpose. But a consultation could be useful to identify the problems such a closure could cause and whether there are adequate alternative arrangements. The problems will arise if the public believe they are being asked whether the unit should close or not.

The interim report of the NHS Next Stage Review, prepared by Professor Lord Ara Darzi and issued in October 2007, emphasised the need to:

- "Ensure that any major change in the pattern of local NHS hospital services is clinically led and locally accountable, by publishing new guidelines to make clear that change should only be initiated when there is a clear and strong clinical basis for doing so;

- Consultation should proceed only where there is effective and early engagement with the public;

- Resources are made available to open new facilities alongside old ones closing."

Generally speaking, consultation, if it is to be properly done, requires time, effort and resources. One of the problems facing organisations such as LINks (The Local Involvement Network) which try to involve the public is that they are seriously under-resourced. Their 'Enter and View' groups which scrutinise NHS and social care services provide a valuable contribution, but as a vehicle for involving the public they are competing with the mechanisms of both the local authority and the commissioning groups. There needs to be proper coordination between the various agencies attempting to involve the public so that resources can be affectively used.

The theme which emerges from this piece of work, however, is that involvement should be 'positive', not merely 'passive'. People should be playing an active part in promoting schemes for healthy living and reducing the risk of conditions such as diabetes and cancer, and also helping to provide support for those requiring long-term care. Again, I cannot stress too much that such an approach is not 'free'. Sometimes when I hear rhetoric about the 'Big Society' it leaves the impression that public involvement and volunteering is a way of saving money. It will do in the sense of reducing other burdens on the NHS in the longer term, such as preventing illness, and stopping unnecessary periods in hospital. The process itself however, will require proper support. It is easy to be idealistic about involvement, particularly in more deprived areas. Groups need support with such things as doing the minutes, finances need to be properly organised, and there have to be procedures to prevent the misappropriation of funds, whether deliberate or not.

Here again there needs to be a change of culture by both government and the NHS. Groups which care for those with long-term conditions may need to agitate on their behalf, to draw attention to ways they may be excluded from society, or simply for more resources, and they must be free to do so. Similarly, the most effective campaigns to reduce ill health, such as Fresh, although publicly funded have been free to operate independently and involve many different agencies. Public money must be properly accounted for, but groups need to be free to act independently. There is also the issue of the actual status of volunteers. Many complain that they are not treated seriously by professionals, and this is often the case, and I can understand why. Some volunteers are unreliable and do not take what they are doing seriously. Others are concerned about promoting particular issues. Volunteers need to be properly recruited, and understand their obligations. In return they must be given proper expenses, and even possibly some sort of honorarium for their work. There also needs to be training. This does put some responsibility on the NHS or voluntary organisations. If volunteers do not perform effectively there must also be a way of improving their performance, or if necessary, removing them. There needs to be a professional relationship.

So far the emphasis has been on community health, on long-term care and promoting healthy lifestyles. I have not mentioned the Foundation Trusts. I was impressed by the effort that the Northumbria Trust had put into both building up its membership and effectively involving them. Others could learn from this. Again, there needs to be a real commitment by the people who run the Foundation Trust. Some appear to have recruited members simply because they had to, and not thought very hard about what to do with them after that. They need to learn from good practice elsewhere.

## Changing the boundaries between community and acute health

The boundaries between community and acute health are becoming less clear cut. In many parts of the country there is an 'integrated pathway' where community and acute services are managed by the same trust. If this is the same boundary as the local authority, the scope for integration of activities, particularly involving the public, are much enhanced. In some areas the boundaries are rather messy. The area where I live, for example, is split between three acute hospitals. The community services are managed by one, but most people in my town go to another. These anomalies need to be removed as far as possible.

This book has not dealt with the details of the economics of the NHS except to appreciate that whatever regime is in place the demands on it will increase and funding will always be finite. The ideas set out envisage a shift from acute to community medicine. But we have to remember the actual distribution of the NHS budget. The amount allocated to public health as part of the total

NHS budget is small – something like 4%, and the total budget for social care is £17 billion for 2010-11 (DoH), compared to a total NHS budget for last year of £114 billion. The majority of the resources are still devoted to acute care or hospitals (although GPs will be using an increasing proportion of their 'slice' of the budget to commission services locally).

It will mean the closure of some district general hospitals, and the use of more community ones as hubs for community services. The sophisticated acute medicine, which is becoming increasingly hi-tech and expensive, will be performed in fewer regional centres, and this does present problems of access, particularly for those without cars. The NHS and local government will have to think about this. Buses are not always the answer. People will often not use them in case they miss the last one home. Taxi contracts could turn out to be more economic.

There will be ferocious campaigns against closure or what the public perceive as 'downgrading' of much loved local hospitals. Public engagement will be very important here – the issues must be clearly explained clearly and honestly to people so that they understand what is happening, but as Professor Darzi pointed out, other provision must be in place before closures happen. A&E is a particular problem. It simply is not possible to maintain an adequate range of qualified A&E staff in many smaller hospitals.

## Best practice

People need to have some clear vision of what an NHS in the future would look like. It is important to look at current good practice to see what can be done. The example of Northumberland is a good one. This is a large rural county with several small hospitals. I described this in Chapter 6, and the model they are aiming for is a network of community hospitals with a modern acute hospital as the hub.

For those not familiar with the area, the Trust covers a large rural area, an industrial ex-coalmining area in South East Northumberland, and the urban area of North Tyneside. The new A&E facility will be at the junction of several main roads. All 'blue light' cases will go to the new Emergency Care Hospital.

Regarding successful consultations, the one over Bishop Auckland by the County Durham Health and Social Care Overview and Scrutiny Committee is a good example.[87] This was very resource-intensive and took over six months. It came to the conclusion that it was not possible to maintain three district hospitals in Durham providing a range of services, but that the health authorities should consider:

- "The need to ensure that services are developed as close to people's homes and in their communities – investing in community hospitals and other community based health and social care provision planned in partnership with social care providers and voluntary and community agencies;

- The need to invest in services at Bishop Auckland General Hospital (BAGH) to ensure future sustainability including establishing a centre of excellence for rehabilitation, investment in stroke services that are delivered alongside rehabilitation services, and central haematology and pathology services (diagnostic services)."

*(Durham County Council, 'Seizing the Future', 2008)*

Bishop Auckland is a long-established District Hospital serving some remote areas in the Durham Dales. The Co Durham and Darlington Foundation Trust also administers two larger hospitals which are more centrally situated in the county. The consultation was about taking away A&E from Bishop Auckland and making it more of a community hospital. It had previously been a centre of excellence for stroke services, and the idea of a rehabilitation services was supported by a campaign by a patient involvement group (Durham and Darlington CPPIH). Nevertheless, the idea of closing the A&E was not popular. Painstaking work by the committee, including a visit by Professor Alberti resulted in acceptance of the change with certain safeguards. The whole process required considerable work by members and officers. This is how scrutiny should be done. The case was honestly presented and the Trust was prepared to engage with the public.

# Privatisation

There remains one issue which this book has not considered in depth, but which has to be addressed. That is privatisation. This is not such an issue in the North East where most health provision is public, and contains some nationally and even internationally regarded hospitals such as the Freeman and the Royal Victoria Infirmary. But it is a concern, and haphazard privatisation could undermine the whole vision being articulated here.

The present government believes public provision is often inefficient and wasteful, and private provision delivers a better service. Although there may be examples where this is the case, I am not aware of any evidence that it is automatically always true, any more than saying it always rains at Blackpool because it sometimes does. What advocates of privatisation often mean is that public services are badly managed, and that unions are too powerful. There may be examples where this is true, but if it is, privatisation is not necessarily the way to deal with these problems. The NHS is actually very efficient in terms of delivering outcomes because of the strong central control of budgets. Systems which are insurance-based, notably the USA, spend more on healthcare without delivering better outcomes. Much is spent on lawyers' fees and administration rather than front-line care.

The vision I have articulated requires cooperation between health professionals and local government, and involvement of the wider community. This would be difficult if the service were fragmented, and particularly difficult if the commissioning organisation which will be responsible to the GPs is privatised. This is the real issue about privatisation. The new commissioning groups will rely on the commissioning organisation to provide them with information and advice. It must be something in which they have confidence and also which they control.

I am aware that the NHS (and local authorities) will use private and third sector providers for some services which they cannot provide themselves, and there has to be an alternative provider if a service does not perform properly. In many cases privatisation consists of a different management controlling the existing workforce. When local government or NHS services do not perform well it is frequently because of bad management rather than the front line staff. This is what is happening at Hinchinbrooke Hospital[88]. In such cases, there is usually a contract for a specific period and the pay and conditions of the staff are protected by TUPE.[89] The use of the private sector under the previous government was largely to provide finance for the building of new hospitals (the Private Finance Initiative, or PFI). This has been criticised as not providing value for money, and in Northumberland the health trust has been loaned £100 million to release it from a 'crippling' PFI deal involving Hexham and Wansbeck hospitals.[90]

In the last resort, service users cannot be sacrificed for the benefit of ideology. But to ensure control over the process, and proper working between the local authority and the NHS, the commissioning organisation could become a social enterprise jointly owned by the GP commissioning groups and the local authority. At the moment these commissioning organisations are the part of the PCT which has not been transferred to the local authority for public health. But given the ideology of the present government this is something where the large private organisations would try and move in. Once such an organisation is privatised, there could well be a presumption to recommending private providers. The new GP and local government organisa-tions will rely on the commissioning organisation for advice, so it is crucial for this to remain a public body. It could become a social enterprise, jointly owned by the local authority and the GPs. This is a move a new government would have to make fairly quickly. Those who want a privatised NHS may try to expedite the process before the next election.

The last Labour government put a cap of 15% on the amount of privatisation in the NHS. This allowed the use of private contrac-tors when it was necessary, and also allowed the NHS the option to bring in the private sector to manage an organisation when it was failing as a last resort. Nevertheless, the overall direction of policy was a publicly-owned NHS, and such a public declaration gave a vote of confidence to the majority of the workforce who are committed to working for the public. A future Labour govern-ment should reinstate such a commitment.

## The need for political will

There is one more point which I am sure many readers will raise. The thrust of my argument is that effectively involving more people in the management of the NHS, and integrating health more with local government will both revive local government and lead to a more publicly accountable health service. What if the local government is run by people who do not want good public services? What if we ended up with a situation like Wisconsin in 2012 where the Tea Party governor Scott Walker is setting out to decimate public services?

This is a perpetual dilemma for those who believe in more local democracy and accountability in a country with a centralised system of government. A National Health Service ensures good standards everywhere. What if right-wing local authorities either reduced or privatised it? Government may have to consider minimum standards. The aim of greater involvement is to improve health, and it should become an essential part of the NHS's culture, rather than a political issue.

This chapter has attempted to draw together the conclusions of the preceding ones. The final one will set out a programme for an incoming government committed to both local government and the NHS.

*This chapter sets out a vision of a publicly-owned health service committed to serving the public. Its objectives will not be simply to provide healthcare, but also to actively reduce health inequalities. To do so it is imperative to involve the public far more than is currently done. Health inequalities can only be addressed at a grassroots level by mobilising the public to promote healthy living and to assist with long term care.*

*The existing mechanisms of the NHS enable a vigorous management which believes in involvement to promote it, and there are examples here in the North East where this has been done. The Health and Wellbeing Boards give an opportunity for the NHS and local government to work more closely together, to involve people more and to provide democratic accountability.*

*The vision is of a publicly-owned NHS, accountable to the public. I recognise that sometimes the private sector needs to be used, but there needs to be an overall commitment to a publicly-run service. Commissioning organisations should be publicly owned, and accountable to clinical commissioning groups and local authorities. To preserve morale in the publicly run service a cap on private commissioning is suggested, as the previous Labour government imposed.*

*Finally some local government may be ideologically opposed to providing good public services, and a future government must ensure basic standards to guard against local government involvement leading to a deterioration in services.*

# CHAPTER 11

# THE WAY FORWARD

THIS BOOK is aimed at those who believe in the philosophy of our NHS, but want to take it forward in the future. I am hoping that a future Labour government, or one in which Labour plays a leading role, will be able to implement these ideas. I hope too, that the book will be of interest to a wider audience which will contain many professionals involved in health and social care, in local government, and in politics and public policy more generally. Members of the Labour Party and some Liberal Democrats will support the whole concept of the NHS, but I hope some Conservatives who follow ideas of 'civil association' as expressed in Oakeshott's last major work on politics, 'On Human Conduct', [91] will find it interesting too. Oakeshott's ideas are regarded by many as being behind the concept of the 'Big Society'. What the book sets itself against is the idea that health is a business, or a commodity to be bought and sold, rather than something which involves all of us. In fact, many would regard the NHS as a practical expression of our national identity.

We live in a world of globalisation and upheaval, and it sometimes appears that there is no longer any room for basic principles in public and political life. I profoundly believe this is not so. Principles must be capable of realisation, or they will not be of much use to those in the practical business of making society work. The principles behind the NHS were basically collective, that health is a responsibility of the whole of society, and we all have a duty to contribute.

Concern is often expressed that in a more individualistic and materialistic society, values of community and solidarity are hard to sustain. We have in the NHS an example of where they have been sustained for more than sixty years. The reason that so many people feel so passionately about the NHS is that they feel these values are being abandoned in the pursuit of the market and private profit. Recent revelations of corruption in high places have, if anything, strengthened this belief.

Many features of our everyday life remind us of how important the NHS is to our lives. I am a regular at the swimming baths, where many of us of a certain age go to keep ourselves tolerably fit, and to have a good gossip. If one of the regulars is missing, it is usually because he or she has to go to hospital for some treatment or an operation. Although many may be nervous about the operation there is never any fear about the financial consequences. They are usually back again after recuperation, and their experiences form the staple of conversation for the next few days. In terms of human happiness, the NHS has done a great deal for all of us.

But to believe in the NHS does not mean it can be frozen in time, nor does it mean not acknowledging that it is sometimes badly managed, or can make mistakes. Most importantly as a major public service it does not seem to have got its relationship with the wider public, its owners and users, right.

This book addresses two issues, which are interlinked. One is that the pressure on the NHS will increase, but the resources to fund it are finite, and it is no use pretending they are not. The other is that it needs to be more closely linked with the wider public, and in particular local government. The two are interlinked because the need to address the health problems we face, and use resources effectively, will mean the transfer of resources from acute hospitals into the community, and this may involve the closure, or conversion, of some hospitals. This is always a difficult issue, and can only really be addressed if the NHS is honest with the public, explains the issues to the public, and is willing to engage in a productive debate with them. Local politicians need to engage as well, and not simply try to gain short-term popularity by opposing very change of use or closure of a facility. If we are to be successful in dealing with the major challenges linked to unhealthy lifestyles such as cancer and diabetes, then we must have the public onside too. If we do not these problems will come back to bite us not only in terms of human misery, but crippling costs for the NHS as well.

We do not know what state the economy and the NHS will be in at the time of the next election, or what the complexion of the next government will be. I sincerely hope that the NHS will be a major issue at that election, and the country can make a decision as to whether it wants to continue with a National Health Service, involving all of us, free at the point of use, but expecting obligations from us as well, or move towards some sort of insurance-based privatised system, as some big vested interests seem to want.

I am optimistic. Big business carried all before it in the last decade of the 20th and first decade of this century, delivering wealth which was unequally distributed but still sufficient to pay for improvements in health and other social goods such as housing, schools and railways. Now the system has proved to be unable to deliver in the long term, as thinkers as diverse as Adam Smith and Marx pointed out in the past, and is being challenged all over the world. Even Rupert Murdoch, the high priest of unfettered financial power who thought he could ignore governments, has been called to account. I do not think the British people will want to entrust such a precious commodity as health to the vagaries of big business. But it is not enough just to have an enthusiasm for the NHS. Unless we have a clear way forward the system will not be able to deliver and people will become disillusioned.

Because it does express such deep moral values, political support is easy to mobilise to defend the NHS, so we must make it clear that although it may sometimes need to use the private sector, the system is not going to be privatised, and some form of individual health insurance established. We will still have a collective national health system.

Demands on the NHS will increase. The population is aging, medicine and medical equipment will become more expensive, and the consequences of 'lifestyle' diseases, such as diabetes, coronary heart disease and some cancers, unless they are addressed, will add further costs.

A future government will therefore need to:

- Protect NHS budgets in real terms, and expand them as resources allow.

- Mobilise volunteers in a professional way to deal with problems of unhealthy lifestyles and long-term care.

- Ensure that local government, the voluntary sector and the NHS work together effectively.

- Ensure that the public are effectively involved in the direction of policy, particularly when difficult decisions have to be made, as they will have to be.

- Prohibit the privatisation of commissioning organisations, ensuring they become social enterprises jointly owned by commissioning groups and local authorities.

- Put a cap, as the previous Labour government did, on the percentage of services which can be provided by private contractors. There must be an overall commitment to the public sector, provided it is properly run.

- Require Foundation Trusts to reach demanding targets for membership and effective involvement of members, learning from the good practice of successful ones.

- Enable successful Foundation Trusts and Commissioning Groups to take over poorly performing ones. Public ownership should not mean a tolerance of inefficiency.

- Separate the roles of acute trusts for serious cases, and community hospitals for less serious ones, recuperation, respite, and preventative work. Community hospitals will work with the wider community and GPs.

- Be prepared to face the fact that some district general hospitals are neither one nor the other, and reorganisation may be required. The NHS and local government will have to show leadership, and effective engagement as described above. Resources have to be spent where they can be most effectively used.

- Free up acute beds in the specialist hospitals by providing more 'step down' facilities in the community for those who do not need acute treatment, but have not recovered sufficiently to be completely discharged. This will make it much easier to engage with their own families and communities.

This is not meant to be a comprehensive list, but a contribution to debate. I hope others will join in the debate with contributions about other aspects of health which I have not touched on here. Politicians, both local and national, must be prepared to show leadership in making firm commitments to a publicly owned and funded NHS, but also be prepared to engage in real debate about how it needs to change for the future. A clear unequivocal commitment to a publicly owned NHS, involving and serving the public, should be an election winner as well as being morally right. For once, the two concerns of the Labour Party, principle and winning, are not in conflict but coincide.

# REFERENCES

## Chapter 1

(1)    Lawson, N. (1992) The View from No.11: Memoirs of a Tory Radical. London: Bantam Press.

(2)    Health and Social Care Act 2012, London: HMSO.

## Chapter 2

(3)    The NHS Constitution 2012, London: Department of Health.

(4)    World Health Organisation, Constitution, Geneva 2011.

(5)    *The Marmot Review*, 'Fair Society, Healthy Lives', University College London, Institute of Health Equity, 2010.

(6)    Health and Social Care Bill, Amendments Considered in Committee, Tuesday 5th July, 2011, *Hansard*.

(7)    There is a useful summary of the work of the public health pioneers in 'New Public Health', by John Ashton and Howard Seymour (1 Dec 1988).

(8)    White Paper: 'Healthy lives, healthy people: our strategy for public health in England', Department of Health, 30 November 2010.

(9)    Department of Health (2003) Tackling health inequalities: A Programme for Action. London: HMSO.

(10) Wilkinson, R. and Pickett, K. (2009) The Spirit Level: Why Equality is Better for Everyone. London: Alan Lane.

(11) Ginsberg, N. (1992) Divisons of Welfare. London: Sage.

(12) Independent Inquiry into Care Provided by Mid Staffordshire NHS Foundation Trust January 2005 – March 2009, Chaired by Robert Francis QC, NHS 2010.

## Chapter 3

(13) Timmins, N. (1995) The Five Giants: A Biography of the Welfare State. London: Harper Collins.

(14) Webster, C. (2002) The National Health Service: a Political History. Oxford: Oxford University Press.

(15) Glasby, J., Peck, E., Ham, C. and Dickinson, H. (2007) Things can only get better? The argument for NHS independence. Birmingham: University of Birmingham.

(16) Hunter, D.J., Marks, L. and Smith, K.E. (2010) The Public Health System in England. Cambridge: The Policy Press.

(17) Elcock, H. (1994) Local Government, Policy and Management in Local Authorities. London: Routledge.

(18) National Health Service and Community Care Act 1990, London: HMSO.

(19) Henderson, M. (2001) Managing in Health and Social Care. London: Routledge.

(20) Martin, V., Charlesworth, J. and Henderson, M. (2010) Managing in Health and Social Care (2nd edition). London: Routledge.

(21) Weber, M. (trans. 1947) The Theory of Economic and Social Organisations. Chicago: The Free Press.

(22) Du Gay, P. (2000) In Praise of Bureaucracy. London: Sage.

(23) Miner, J.B. (2007) Organisational Behaviour: Theory to Practice. NY: ME Sharp.

(24) Handy, C.B. (2009) Understanding Organisations (revised 4th edition) Harmondsworth: Penguin Books Limited.

(25) Wood, J.C. and Wood, M.C. (2002) F.W. Taylor: Critical Evaluations in Business and Management. London: Taylor and Francis.

(26) Hoggett, P. (1991) A new management in the public sector. *Policy and Politics* 19, 4: 143-56.

(27) Bolton, S.C. (2004) A Simple Matter of Control? NHS Hospital Nurses and New Management. *Journal of Management Studies* 41, (2) 317 – 333.

(28) Drucker, P.F. (1992) Managing the Non-Profit Organisation, Practices and Principles. London: Butterworth-Heinemann. (2008) The Five Most Important Questions You Will Ever Ask About Your Organisation. NY: Jossey-Bass.

(29) Peston, R. (2008) Who Runs Britain? London: Hodder and Stoughton.

(30) Sennett, R. (1998) The Corrosion of Character, Yale: Yale University Press. (2007) The Culture of the New Capitalism. Yale: Yale University Press.

(31) Harrison, B. (1994) Lean and Mean. Guilford: Guilford University Press.

(32) NHS Choices is a website run by the NHS to enable patients to make informed choices.

(33) Klein, R. The new politics of the NHS from creation to reinvention. Oxford: Radcliffe Publishing.

(34) Exworthy, M. and Halford, S. (1999) Professionals and managers in a changing public sector: conflict, compromise and collaboration. Basingstoke: Open University Press.

(35) National Health Service and Community Care Act (1990). London: HMSO.

(36) 'Our Health, Our Care, Our Say' A new direction for community services (2006) London: HMSO.

(37) Health Investor Magazine (2012) March 22nd 2012, London: Investor Publishing.

(38) Darzi, A. (2005) Acute Services Review – Hartlepool and Teeside. London: Department of Health.

(39) Harrison, R. (1972) What Kind of Organisation? Development Research Associates. London: McGraw Hill.

(40) Hudson, B. (2004) Whole Systems Working: Discussion Paper for the Integrated Care Network; Analysing Network Partnerships, Public Management Review 6 (1):75-94.

(41) Florin, D. and Dixon, J. (2004) Public involvement in health care. British Medical Journal, 328:159 -161.

(42) Baggott, R. (2005) A Funny Thing Happened on the Way to the Forum? Reforming Patient and Public Involvement in the NHS in England. Public Administration 83 (3) 533-551.

(43) Arnstein, S. (1969) A Ladder of Citizen Participation. Journal of the American Planning Association, Vol 35, No 4, pp 216-224.

(44) Hudson, B. (2006) Whole Systems Working: A Guide and Discussion Paper. NHS Care Services Improvement Partnership, Integrated Care Network. London: Department of Health.

(45) Hudson, B. and Henwood, M. (2008) Lost in the System? London: CSCI.

(46) Langton, C.G. (1990) Artificial Life, Proceedings of the Santa Fe Institute Studies in the Science of Complexity, Vol 6 Redwood City, CA. Addison-Wesley.

(47) Cooper, Z., Gibbons, S., Jones, S. & McGuire, A. (2010) Does Hospital Competition Improve Efficiency? An Analysis of the Recent Market-Based Reforms to the English NHS. London: London School of Economics.

## Chapter 4

(48) Levitt, R. (1980) Consumers, Community Health Councils and the NHS. London: Kings Fund Centre.

(49) Kennedy, I. (2001) The Kennedy Report: Learning from Bristol: the report of the public inquiry into children's heart surgery at the Bristol Royal Infirmary 1984 – 1995. Command Paper CM 5207 London.

(50) Robbins, M. (2006) Medical Secretaries and Receptionists Handbook, Fourth Edition. Oxford: Radcliffe Publishing.

(51) BBC News, 15 October 2007. Many 'cannot get NHS dental care', Report on survey into dentistry by the Commission for Patient and Public Involvement in Health (CPPIH).

(52) For a wide-ranging review of the Scottish arrangements, see Review of Community Health Partnerships prepared by Audit Scotland in June 2011.

(53) Care Quality Commission (2011) Preparing for HealthWatch: CQC's plan to set up HealthWatch England. Care Quality Commission, Newcastle upon Tyne.

(54) Darzi, A. (2008) Our NHS, Our Future. NHS Next Stage Review Leading Local Change. London: Department of Health.

## Chapter 5

(55) Department of the Environment, Transport and the Regions (1998) Making the Difference, A New Start for England's Coalfield Communities. London: HMSO.

(56) Smith, P. (2010) Social and Educational Initiatives in East Durham between 1985 and 2005: Perceptions and Experiences. Sunderland University.

(57) Communities and Local Government Committee (2010) Beyond Decent Homes: fourth report of session 2009-10 Vol 1. *Hansard*. London: HMSO.

(58) Townsend, P., Phillimore, P. and Beattie, A. (1987) Health Deprivation: Inequality in the North. Beckenham: Croom Helm; (1994) Inequalities in Health in the North East Region. Northern Regional Health Authority and University of Bristol.

(59) Walker, G.A. (2009) The Peter Townsend Reader. Cambridge: The Policy Press.

(60) MacDonald, Dr Stephen and Taylor-Gooby, David (2010) The Role of Public and Patient Involvement in Practice Based Commissioning within Easington NHS Services. University of Sunderland Centre for Children, Young People and Families.

(61) For a full description of the Hospital of God, its organisation and history, consult the website. www.hospitalofgod.org.uk

(62) A full description of Healthworks is given on the County Durham and Darlington PCT website: www.health-improvement.cdd.nhs.uk. Future readers should note that responsibility for this project may change with the NHS reforms. The healthworks model has been followed elsewhere.

## Chapter 6

(63) The International Cooperative Alliance has issued a modern version of these in 1995 – 'The Statement of Cooperative Identity'. International Cooperative Alliance, Geneva, Switzerland.

(64) Lewis, Richard and Hinton, Lisa (2005) Putting Health in Local Hands: Early Experiences of Homerton University Hospital NHS Foundation Trust. London: The Kings Fund.

(65) Day, P. and Klein, R. (2005) Governance of Foundation Trusts. London: The Nuffield Trust.

(66) Verzulli, R., Jacobs, R., and Goddard, M. (2011) Do hospitals respond to greater autonomy? Evidence from the

English NHS. Paper 64, York University, Centre for Health Economics.

(67) Nuffield Foundation Website, July 11th 2011. Abstract of the research.

(68) Northumbria Trust website: www.northumbria.nhs.uk

## Chapter 7

(69) Wilkinson, R. and Pickett, K. (2009) op. cit.

(70) Bambra, Clare (May 2012) Clear Winners and Losers from age only resource allocation. British Medical Journal, London: May 26th 2012.

(71) Taylor-Gooby, P. (2012) A Left Trilemma. London: Policy Network.

(72) Whitehead, M. (author), Townsend, P. and Davidson, N. (editors) (1982) Inequalities in Health: The Black Report and the Health Divide. London: Penguin.

(73) Dr Taylor was MP for Wyre Forest from 2001 to 2010. He campaigned solely on the issue of the closure of the A&E department at Kidderminster hospital.

(74) Fresh was the UK's first dedicated regional programme set up in the North East of England in 2005 to tackle the worst rates of smoking-related illness and death in the country. For further information consult the website: http://www. freshne.com/

(75) Russel, A. et al (2009) The evolution of a UK regional tobacco control office in its early years: social contexts and policy dynamics. Health Promotion International, Vol. 24 No.3. Oxford: Oxford University Press.

(76) Balance is the North East of England's Alcohol Office – and the first of its kind in the UK established in 2009. Its website http://www.balancenortheast.co.uk states "We are aiming to inspire changes to the way people in the North East think

about and drink alcohol. We aren't saying no to alcohol and we still want people to enjoy themselves. But we do want to encourage people to reduce their consumption – and reduce the impact that alcohol is having on our region."

(77) Foot, J. and Hopkins, T. (2010) A glass half full: how an asset based approach can improve community health and wellbeing. London Improvement and Development Agency.

(78) For a full discussion of co-production and what it means in health and social care see Loeffler, E., Taylor-Gooby, D., Bovaird, T., Hine-Hughes, F. and Wilkes, L. (editors) (2012) Making Health and Social Care Personal and Local Moving from Mass Production to Co-production. Birmingham: Governance International.

## Chapter 8

(79) BMA General Practitioners Committee (September 2011) Health and Wellbeing Boards GP Guidance. London: British Medical Association.

(80) HM Treasury and Department of Communities and Local Government (March 2010) Total place: a whole area approach to public services. London: HMSO.

(81) Ham, C. et al (2011) Where Next for the NHS Reforms? London: The Kings Fund.

(82) Durham County Council (December 2008) Response to the public consultation on Seizing the Future – proposals for NHS service reconfiguration in County Durham and Darlington. Durham.

## Chapter 9

(83) The OECD is the Organisation for Economic Cooperation and Development. Its website states: "Our origins date back to 1960, when 18 European countries plus the United States and Canada joined forces to create an organisation dedicated to global development. Today, our 34 member

countries span the globe, from North and South America to Europe and the Asia-Pacific region. They include many of the world's most advanced countries but also emerging countries like Mexico, Chile and Turkey. We also work closely with emerging giants like China, India and Brazil and developing economies in Africa, Asia, Latin America and the Caribbean. Together, our goal continues to be to build a stronger, cleaner, fairer world."

(84) Wilkinson and Pickett (2009) op cit.

(85) 'Sir Len Fenwick fights to save Tyneside eye screening programme' Newcastle Journal July 11th 2012. http://www.journallive.co.uk/north-east-news/todays-news/2012/07/11/sir-len-fenwick-fights-to-save-tyneside-eye-screening-programme-61634-31372098/#ixzz2ozKZKy6n

## Chapter 10

(86) Diabetes UK (May 2012) The State of the Nation 2012. London: Diabetes UK.

(87) Durham County Council December 2008, op cit.

(88) In February 2012, Hinchingbrooke became the first NHS hospital to be operated by a private partner. Hinchingbrooke remains an NHS hospital, delivering NHS services, while its staff, building and assets remain in the NHS. (http://www.hinchingbrooke.nhs.uk/)

(89) TUPE is the acronym for The Transfer of Undertakings (Protection of Employment) Regulations 2006. These are the United's implementation of the European Union Business Transfers Directive [1]. It is an important part of UK labour law, protecting employees whose business is being transferred to another business. The 2006 regulations replace the old 1981 regulations.

(90) David Black, The Journal, February 27th 2012.

## Chapter 11

(91) Oakeshott, M.J. (1975) On Human Conduct. London: Clarendon Press.

Lightning Source UK Ltd.
Milton Keynes UK
UKOW041326160413

209297UK00001B/31/P